*Frontispiece:* Stamped centerpiece of helmeted man from the Classic Christian period

*Publications of the Pennsylvania-Yale Expedition to Egypt*

WILLIAM KELLY SIMPSON, *Director and Editor*

Number 3

# THE CLASSIC CHRISTIAN TOWNSITE AT ARMINNA WEST

*by Kent R. Weeks*

*Based on field work, notes, and plans by the author and the director, and*

*Peter Mayer*

*Albert Sandleben*

*Charles Seymour III*

*Reinhard Huber*

*Aubrey S. Trik*

THE PEABODY MUSEUM OF NATURAL HISTORY OF YALE UNIVERSITY

THE UNIVERSITY MUSEUM OF THE UNIVERSITY OF PENNSYLVANIA

*New Haven and Philadelphia*

*1967*

## Expedition Staff 1963

| | |
|---|---|
| DIRECTOR | WILLIAM KELLY SIMPSON |
| DEPUTY DIRECTOR | AUBREY S. TRIK |
| CHIEF ARCHAEOLOGIST | KENT R. WEEKS |
| ARCHITECTS | PETER MAYER |
| | ALBERT SANDLEBEN |
| DRAFTSMAN | REINHARD HUBER |
| FIELD ASSISTANTS | CHARLES SEYMOUR III |
| | WILLIAM PENNELL ROCK (*1st half*) |
| | ROBERT GIEGENGACK (*2d half*) |
| | PAUL EYANSON (*2d half*) |
| INSPECTOR | MOHAMMED SALIH |

## Laboratory Staff 1965

| | |
|---|---|
| ARTIST | SUSAN L. HOWE |
| CERAMIC TYPOLOGY STUDY | CHARLES SEYMOUR III |
| | JEFFREY D. JENNINGS |
| | KATHERINE DAVENNY |
| | CORNELIUS J. DWYER |

# Contents

# List of Figures, Tables, and Plates

*A Note on the Figures*

*The illustrations which accompany the ceramic study are based upon materials from the Arminna West Classic Christian Townsite and the classifications of William Y. Adams. We have altered some of his vessel illustrations to conform to variations in form at Arminna West, but have generally conformed to his published descriptions. Numbers accompanying each vessel, if found in Adams' classification, are his sub-form numbers. Other numbers and letters refer to the location of a particular vessel in the Townsite. Numbers enclosed by a square are strata designations, while those in circles are Pennsylvania-Yale catalogue numbers.*

## FIGURES

## TABLES

PLATES

# Abbreviations

*ASN* *The Archaeological Survey of Nubia, Reports* and *Bulletins,* Cairo, 1909–1927.

*Bull. Soc. Geog. d'Eg.* *Bulletin de la Société de Géographie d'Égypte,* Cairo.

*Expedition* *Expedition, The Bulletin of the University Museum of the University of Pennsylvania,* Philadelphia.

*ILN* *Illustrated London News,* London.

*JARCE* *Journal of the American Research Center in Egypt,* Boston.

*JEA* *Journal of Egyptian Archaeology,* London.

*Kush* *Kush, Journal of the Sudan Antiquities Service,* Khartoum.

*LAAA* *Liverpool Annals of Archaeology and Anthropology,* Liverpool.

*Serv. des Antiq., Mission de Nubie* *Service des Antiquités de l'Égypte, Mission Archéologique de Nubie,* 1929–34, Cairo.

*SNR* *Sudan Notes and Records,* Khartoum.

*Sudan Antiq. Serv., O.P.* *Sudan Antiquities Service, Occasional Papers,* Khartoum.

# Literature Cited

Adams, William Y. "The Christian Potteries at Faras," *Kush* IX (1961): 30–43.

— "The Archaeological Survey on the West Bank of the Nile: Second Season, 1960–1," *Kush* X (1962): 10–18.

— "Pottery Kiln Excavations," *Kush* X (1962): 62–75.

— "An Introductory Classification of Christian Nubian Pottery," *Kush* X (1962): 245–88.

— "An Introductory Classification of Meroitic Pottery," *Kush* XII (1964): 126–73.

— "Sudan Antiquities Service Excavations in Nubia: Fourth Season, 1962–63," *Kush* XII (1964): 216–48.

— "Post-Pharaonic Nubia in the Light of Archaeology," *JEA* 50 (1964): 102–20; 51 (1965): 160–78.

— "Sudan Antiquities Service Excavations at Meinarti, 1963–64," *Kush* XIII (1965): 148–76.

— and Hans-Åke Nordström. "The Archaeological Survey on the West Bank of the Nile: Third Season, 1961–62," *Kush* XI (1963): 10–46.

Almagro, M., F. Presedo, and M. Pellicer. "Preliminary Report on the Spanish Excavations in the Sudan, 1961–62," *Kush* XI (1963): 175–95.

— and R. Blanco Caro, M. A. Garcia-Guinea, F. Presedo Velo, M. Pellicer Catalan, and J. Teixidor. "Excavations by the Spanish Archaeological Mission in the Sudan, 1962–63 and 1963–64," *Kush* XIII (1965): 78–95.

Arkell, A. J. "A Christian Church and Monastery at Ain Farah, Darfur," *Kush* VII (1959): 115–19.

— *A History of the Sudan to 1821.* London. Second ed., 1961.

Armelagos, G. J., G. H. Ewing, D. L. Greene and K. K. Greene. "Report of the Physical Anthropology Section, University of Colorado Nubian Expedition," *Kush* XIII (1965): 24–27.

Butler, Alfred J. *The Ancient Coptic Churches of Egypt.* Two vols. Oxford, 1884.

Butzer, Karl W. "Remarks on the Geography of Settlement in the Nile Valley during Hellenistic Times," *Bull. Soc. Géog. d'Égypte* 33 (1960): 5–36.

Christophe, Louis-A. "Remarques sur l'Économie de la Basse-Nubie égyptienne," *Bull. Soc. Géog. d'Égypte* 35 (1963): 77–128.

Crawford, O. G. S. "Castles and Churches in the Middle Nile Region, with a Note on the Inscriptions by M. F. L. Macadam," *Sudan Antiq. Serv. O. P.,* Number 2, 1961.

Crowfoot, J. W. "Christian Nubia," *JEA* 13 (1927): 141–50.

Dunham, Dows, "A Collection of 'Pot-Marks' from Kush and Nubia," *Kush* XIII (1965): 131–47.

Emery, Walter B. "The Royal Tombs of Qustul and Ballana," *Serv. des Antiq., Mission de Nubie, 1929–34.* Two vols. Cairo, 1938.

— *Nubian Treasure.* London, 1948.

— and L. P. Kirwan. "The Excavations and Survey between Wadi es-Sebua and Adindan, 1929–1931," *Serv. des Antiq., Mission de Nubie, 1929–34.* Two vols. Cairo, 1935.

Firth, C. M. *The Archaeological Survey of Nubia, Report for 1908–1909* (2 vols.). Cairo, 1912.

— *The Archaeological Survey of Nubia, Report for 1909–1910.* Cairo, 1915.

— *The Archaeological Survey of Nubia, Report for 1910–1911.* Cairo, 1927.

Griffith, F. L. "Oxford Excavations in Nubia," *LAAA* 8 (1921): 65–104; 9 (1922): 67–124; 10 (1923): 73–171; 11 (1924): 115–25, 141–80; 12 (1925): 57–172; 13 (1926): 17–37, 49–93; 14 (1927): 57–116; 15 (1928): 63–88.

Hewes, Gordon W. "Gezira Dabarosa: Report of the University of Colorado Nubian Expedition, 1962–63 Season," *Kush* XII (1964): 174–87.

Junker, Hermann. *Ermenne: Bericht über die Grabungen der Akademie der Wissenschaften in Wien auf den Friedhöfen von Ermenne (Nubien) im Winter 1911/12.* Akademie der Wissenschaften in Wien, Phil.-hist. Klasse. Denkschr. 67, Bde. 1, Vienne, 1925.

Kammerer, Winifred, E. M. Husselman and L. A. Shier. *A Coptic Bibliography.* Ann Arbor, Mich., 1950.

Kees, Hermann. *Ancient Egypt: A Cultural Topography*. (Ed. by T. G. H. James; trans. by Ian F. D. Morrow). London, 1961.

Kirwan, L. P. "Notes on the Topography of the Christian Nubian Kingdoms," *JEA* 21 (1935): 57–62.

— "Studies in the Later History of Nubia," *LAAA* 24 (1937): 67–105.

MacMichael, H. A. *History of the Arabs in the Sudan*. Two vols. Cambridge, 1922.

Mileham, Geoffrey. *Churches in Lower Nubia*. University of Pennsylvania Egyptian Department of the University Museum, Eckley B. Coxe, Jr., Expedition to Nubia, vol. II. Philadelphia, 1910.

Monneret de Villard, Ugo. *Description générale du Monastère de St. Siméon à Aswan*. Milan, 1927.

— "La Nubia Medioevale," *Serv. des Antiq., Mission de Nubie, 1929–34*. Four vols. Cairo, 1935–57.

— *Storia della Nubia Cristiana. Orientalia Christiana Analecta*, 118. Rome, 1938.

Newell, H. P. and A. D. Krieger. "The George C. Davis Site, Cherokee County, Texas," *Memoirs of the Society for American Archaeology*, number 5. Menasha, Wisconsin, 1949.

Oates, John. "A Christian Inscription in Greek from Armenna in Nubia (Pennsylvania-Yale Excavations)," *JEA* 49 (1963): 161–71.

Presedo Velo, Fransisco J. *Antigüedades Cristianas de la Isla de Kasar-Ico (2a Catarata del Nilo, Sudan)*. Comite Español de la UNESCO para Nubia, Memorias de la Mision Arqueologica, I. Madrid, 1963.

Randall-MacIver, D. and C. L. Woolley. *Areika*. Univ. of Pennsylvania Egyptian Department of the University Museum, Eckley B. Coxe, Jr., Expedition to Nubia, vol. I. Oxford, 1909.

Reisner, G. A. *The Archaeological Survey of Nubia, Report for 1907–1908* (2 vols.). Cairo, 1910.

Shepard, Anna O. *Ceramics for the Archaeologist*. Publication 609 of the Carnegie Institute of Washington. Washington, D.C., 1956.

Shinnie, P. L. "A Note on Some Fragments of Stamped Pottery from Christian Nubia," *SNR* 31 (1950): 297–99.

— "Medieval Nubia," *Sudan Antiq. Serv. Museum Pamphlet*, number 2. Khartoum, 1954.

— "The University of Ghana Excavations at Debeira West," *Kush* XI (1963): 257–63.

— "The University of Ghana Excavations at Debeira West 1963," *Kush* XII (1964): 208–15.

— and H. N. Chittick. "Ghazali—A Monastery in the Northern Sudan," *Sudan Antiq. Serv. O. P.*, number 5. Khartoum, 1961.

Simpson, William Kelly. "In Land which the Waters of the High Dam will Submerge: Discoveries, from Old Kingdom to Coptic Times, at Toshka West," *ILN* 239, no. 6363 (July 15, 1961): 94–95.

— "Expedition to Nubia," *Archaeology* 14, 2 (1961): 213–14.

— "Nubia: The University Museum—Yale University Expedition," *Expedition* IV, 2 (1962): 28–39.

— "Nubia—1962 Excavations at Toshka and Arminna," *Expedition* IV, 4 (1962): 36–46.

— "Yale's Research on the Nile," *Ventures, Magazine of the Yale Graduate School* I (1962): 20–23.

— "Toshka-Arminna: Brief Preliminary Report, Pennsylvania-Yale Archaeological Expedition to Nubia, 1961" *Fouilles en Nubie (1959–61), Campagne Internationale de l'UNESCO pour la Sauvegarde des Monuments de la Nubie*, 41–43. Cairo, 1963.

— "The Pennsylvania-Yale Expedition to Egypt: Preliminary Report for 1963, Toshka and Arminna (Nubia)," *JARCE* III (1964): 15–23.

— *Heka-nefer and the Dynastic Material from Toshka and Arminna. Publications of the Pennsylvania-Yale Expedition to Egypt*, Number 1. New Haven and Philadelphia, 1963.

Smith, H. S. *Preliminary Reports of the Egypt Exploration Society's Nubian Survey*. Cairo, 1952.

Stenico, A. "Ikhmindi, una Città Fortificata Medievale della Bassa Nubia," *Acme* 13 (1960).

Tothill, J. D. (ed.). *Agriculture in the Sudan*. London, 1948.

Trigger, Bruce G. "History and Settlement in Lower Nubia," *Yale University Publications in Anthropology*, number 69. New Haven, 1965.

— *The Late Nubian Settlement at Arminna West. Publications of the Pennsylvania-Yale Expedition to Egypt*, Number 2. New Haven and Philadelphia, 1967.

Vercoutter, Jean. "Ancient Egyptian Influence in the Sudan," *SNR* XL (1959): 8–18.

— "The Gold of Kush: Two Gold-washing Stations at Faras East," *Kush* VII (1959): 120–53.

Weigall, Arthur P. *Antiquities in Lower Nubia in 1906–1907*. Oxford, 1907.

Winlock, H. E., W. E. Crum and Evelyn White. *The Monastery of Epiphanius. Publications of the Metropolitan Museum of Art Egyptian Expedition,* ed. by A. M. Lythgoe. Vols. 3 and 4. New York, 1926.

Woolley, C. L. *Karanog: The Town*. University of Pennsylvania Egyptian Department of the University Museum, Eckley B. Coxe, Jr., Expedition to Nubia, vol. V. Philadelphia, 1911.

— and D. Randall-MacIver. *Karanog: The Romano-Nubian Cemetery. Ibid.*, vols. III, IV. Philadelphia, 1910.

Worrell, William H. *A Short Account of the Copts*. Ann Arbor, Mich., 1945.

# Director's Preface

ARMINNA WEST is the subject of the preceding report by Mr. Trigger, the present report by Mr. Weeks, and a projected report to appear later. Although the site as a whole has been discussed by Trigger (*The Late Nubian Settlement,* pp. 1–4) and Weeks in the present volume (pp. 4–5), an overall description is still required. On the other side of the river from the post boat station in Khor Usha at Arminna East was a prominent brick ruin to the north and south of which the land sloped downward to a plain. The plain was more extensive on the north than on the south, where it was terminated by rocky terrain. The ruin resembled those to the south at er Rammal and Tamit, both sites which had revealed a series of churches. Following earlier visitors to the site, we provisionally regarded it as a monastery.

Our first excavation revealed a series of chambers filled with sand and some sherds and preserved to almost their original height. The surface level approximated that of the partly preserved arched roofs. Our labors consisted of emptying these sand fills to reach the floors and to determine what underlying structures existed. The chambers were of limited interest and did not seem to us to warrant the major task of excavating the entire complex (Area C, 1–8). We were particularly dismayed that the site appeared to have been fairly well cleaned before it was abandoned to the encroaching sands. Our next effort was devoted to an attempt to determine the nature of the complex. To this end Mayer planned the surface walls which could be outlined (fig. 2), and on the basis of the plan we determined to excavate the "Public Building." During the 1963 season the area between the Public Building and our original chambers 1–8 was excavated, all in area C, and in addition a series of chambers abutting on the north of a major east-west wall (fig. 2, Area N). The remainder of the "high town" was left unexcavated as being essentially unpromising. The excavated portion of the high town is the subject of this report by Weeks.

A short distance north of the high town was the area designated as AWH, the subject of Trigger's report. The main features were a Christian church and a series of houses extending from the Meroitic through the X-Group period. A somewhat illegible demotic ostracon was found in the lower levels. Extending for some distance north of this area along the river were the eroded remains of a Meroitic town, not excavated, with some of its house walls preserved to a height of about 30 cm. West of the church and Meroitic townsite, and overlooking them from the nearby ridge, was the interesting but badly plundered cemetery (AWB) which is scheduled to form the subject of our next report. It consisted of the remains of Meroitic superstructures with chapels and modest X-Group tumuli.

In general, I have the impression that the Meroitic occupation was most extensive, with a subsequent diminishment in the population in X-Group times. The Christian occupation was again substantial in some periods, but there was a noticeable shift southward in the microenvironment toward the high town. Toshka West (Sakinya) to the north was the more thriving community at this time, and the installations to the south at er Rammal and Tamit were indeed substantial. Arminna West seems to have occupied a lesser status in the region between these poles. The encroaching sand and perhaps a westward shift of the river put a virtual end to its life.

The Nubian excavations of the Pennsylvania-Yale Expedition to Egypt were made possible through the generous support of the Eckley B. Coxe, Jr. fund of the University Museum of the University of Pennsylvania, a grant from the Bollingen Foundation, established by Mr. Paul Mellon, and a grant from the United States Department of State, Bureau of Educational and Cultural Affairs. I wish to thank Dr. Froelich Rainey, Director of the University Museum, Mr. John D. Barrett, President of the Bollingen Foundation, Dr. S. Dillon Ripley 2d, then Director of the Peabody Museum, and the officers of the Bureau of Educational and Cultural Affairs, particularly Miss Annis Sandvos, for their aid, encouragement, and never failing understanding.

As always, the authorities of the Department of Antiquities of the United Arab Republic have helped us beyond measure: Dr. Anwar Shukry, Director-General, his deputy and successor, Mr. Mohammed Mahdi Ibrahim, Mr. Abdin Siyyam of the Aswan office, and the inspectors assigned to the expedition, who made our work much lighter through their day to day aid and advice, Messrs. Mahir Saleeb, Farouk Gomaa, Kemal Fahmy, and Mohammed Salih.

My indebtedness to various colleagues and to members of the staff of the United States Embassy in Cairo as expressed in the preface to our first monograph is warmly renewed. Mr. James Halsema, Public Affairs Officer, Mr. John Jermain Slocum, Cultural Affairs Officer, and Messrs. Henry Manning and Desmond Jackson, Financial Officers, aided in every conceivable way.

The considerable expenses of this publication have been met by the Coxe funds and the Bollingen grant. In addition publications support has been requested from the National Science Foundation.

I should like to thank Professor Alfred W. Crompton, Director of the Peabody Museum, and the members of the publications committee of the Peabody Museum for their help, and our printers for their considerate cooperation.

WILLIAM KELLY SIMPSON

# Acknowledgments

AN ARCHAEOLOGICAL report of this nature is necessarily the result of the cooperative efforts of many individuals, and to these individuals the author owes a debt of sincere gratitude. If the data presented in this volume have any value, it is due first of all to those members of the Expedition listed above and to their conscientious work in the field and laboratory. The author would particularly like to thank Miss Susan Howe, who prepared all maps and figures for publication, and Mr. Charles Seymour III, who supervised the ceramic typology study, for their unfailing good humor and enthusiasm, even in the face of the author's often incomprehensible directions.

At various times during the course of the work, the author had the opportunity to discuss several problems of archaeological interpretation and Nubian history with scholars whose suggestions have almost without fail been incorporated in the text. Mr. Nicholas B. Millet of the American Research Center in Egypt read and commented upon several chapters. Dr. William Y. Adams offered advice about the ceramic typology. Professor Robert C. Hupton of the Anthropology-Sociology Department, American University in Cairo, read and discussed the manuscript at length. Help was given concerning several questions of methodology by Professors Walter A. Fairservis, Jr., and Robert E. Greengo of the University of Washington, Seattle. Dr. Bruce G. Trigger of McGill University made several valuable suggestions concerning the material discussed in Part 2. To all the author offers his most sincere thanks and credit for whatever of worth may be found herein.

Field work during the 1963 season was under the general supervision of Professor Simpson and, during his absence near the end of the season, was continued by Mr. Aubrey S. Trik.

The photographs of Abu Simbel Village were graciously offered by Mr. Richard Edlund and are included to provide some much-needed ethnographic data for the interpretation of Christian Nubian architectural remains.

The photographs in this volume have been prepared in their final form by Mr. John Howard and his staff in the Photographic Department of the Peabody Museum.

Work on the manuscript was conducted between June, 1965, and May, 1966, in New Haven, Connecticut, Seattle, Washington, and in Cairo. The tiresome and difficult task of typing the manuscript was admirably taken on by Miss Gail Woodward in Cairo.

The author would like to express his deepest thanks to Professor William Kelly Simpson for having given him the opportunity to participate in the Pennsylvania-Yale project at Arminna West, for allowing him to prepare the results of that Expedition for publication, and for having given so freely of his time to offer advice and encouragement.

KENT R. WEEKS

*Cairo*
*June, 1966*

# PART 1

*Introduction:*

# THE PLACE OF ARMINNA WEST IN THE HISTORY OF LOWER NUBIA

BETWEEN THE FIRST and Second Cataracts, the Nile Valley offers a strangely appealing but only rarely hospitable landscape. On the east bank, high rock terraces which drop sharply to the river and show the rugged gashes of intricate wadi systems characterize much of the terrain along this 340 km. stretch of river valley and desert, while on the west bank, areas of wind-blown sand extend to the horizon, occasionally broken by small rock outcroppings. Only in scattered patches of the valley floor is there sufficient silt deposition not covered by sand to allow the growing of crops. Some of these cultivable areas may extend for a kilometer or more, others may be only a few hundred meters square; but in few instances are they sufficient to support the adjacent population.[1]

Since the beginning of the Pleistocene, the geomorphology and ecology of Nubia have undergone several changes. But since the introduction of agriculture, and more particularly since the introduction of the *shaduf* in the New Kingdom and the *saqia* in Hellenistic times, man's utilization of this harsh environment has remained relatively unchanged.[2] His crops have consisted largely of wheat, barley, beans, lentils, and, more recently, maize, and their success has been governed by the variations of the Nile flood. Even with the tools of irrigation his control of nature has been inefficient, and not until the construction of pumping stations during the last few decades could it be said to be more than minimal. His herding activities, too, have been similarly subject, and the cattle, sheep, and goats which he has raised have never offset the often precarious and insufficient crops.

Lower Nubia seems never to have been a truly self-sufficient country, and during much of its history it has been in some way dependent upon the more fertile valley of Egypt for its existence.[3] Yet, despite the apparent poverty of this land, Egypt considered it of no small importance, both for economic and military reasons. The deserts held valuable deposits of copper, gold, diorite, and other materials, and the river served as an important route over which goods could be got from further south. The necessity of protecting this trade, begun as early as the Old Kingdom, and of preventing incursions of various groups from Nubia and adjacent areas into Egypt prompted the construction of several fortresses above the Second Cataract and gave rise to military expeditions as early as Middle Kingdom times.[4] The course of Nubian history has been determined to a very great extent by these two factors: an ecological balance which at best was tenuous, and contact with the north (and with the south, too) which succeeded in influencing elements of its culture from even before Meroitic times to the present day. The material remains of this contact have made possible the chronological framework upon which Nubian history is founded, and some of its aspects are fairly well understood. But a more thorough understanding of this problem and of Nubian cultures in anthropological or better, ethnohistorical, terms is still far from complete.

Until recent years, archaeological research in Egyptian and Sudanese Nubia dealt almost exclusively with materials of a religious or mortuary nature. Through the pioneering studies of the Archaeological Survey of Nubia,[5] the University of Pennsylvania,[6] and such individuals as F. L. Griffith,[7] Monneret de Villard,[8] and Hermann Junker,[9] knowledge of cemeteries, graves and grave goods, mortuary art and architecture, and of religious structures such as churches and temples grew immensely. Yet, despite this early work, our knowledge of the way of life in Nubia remained extremely incomplete. We could fill pages with details of cemetery plans but only few with notes on settlement pattern; we could describe the hierarchy of the Church, but not the social structure of the village. In part, this picture of Nubian cultures was due to the nature of the evidence itself. Texts, for example, have dealt more frequently with sacred matters than with secular. But in part, too, the picture was due to the excavator's preference for mortuary sites, for sites of a type known to have high artifact yield.[10]

1. A convenient summary of the geography of Lower Nubia appears in Trigger, 1965, chap. II.

2. Arkell, 1961. An intensive study of Lower Nubian geology will shortly be available with the publication of R. F. Giegengack's Ph.D. thesis (Yale, 1967).

3. Trigger, 1965. See also Arkell, 1961, Tothill, 1948, and Emery, 1948.

4. Arkell, 1961. Also of importance are the articles by Vercoutter, *Kush* VII (1959) and *SNR* XL (1959). See also Kees, 1961.

5. *ASN, Reports* and *Bulletins,* prepared by Firth, Reisner, Smith, and others, 1909–1927.

6. Woolley, 1911; Woolley and Randall–MacIver, 1910; Randall–MacIver and Woolley, 1909.

7. See especially his reports on the Oxford excavations, *LAAA* VIII–XV (1921–1928).

8. Monneret de Villard, 1935–1957.

9. Junker, 1925.

10. Adams, *Kush* X (1962): 17–18.

In 1960, when plans were being made for an intensive archaeological survey of Nubia prior to the completion of the Saad el Ali, archaeology was still in the throes of a critical self-examination.[11] Developments in anthropology and history and, more generally, the rapid post-war rise of the social sciences gave the archaeologist a different theoretical framework and a new set of problems with which to work. Archaeology was not only an historical tool but was becoming an integral part of the social sciences. It was no longer concerned merely with the retrieval of *objets d'art* or the excavation of large ceremonial structures but attempted to provide historical depth to the study of Man as a sociocultural being.

This "new" theoretical approach, accompanied by numerous methodological changes, had, of course, been utilized in prehistoric studies for several years.[12] But it had yet to be applied with any regularity to studies of the historic period. The archaeological work conducted in Nubia during the last six years has represented one of the first intensive applications of these new theories and techniques to the sociocultural problems of historic cultures in a single area. And one need only examine the studies of William Y. Adams[13] or Bruce G. Trigger[14] or the excavation reports of Nicholas B. Millet[15] to see how successful this approach has already been. Now, in addition to knowledge of art, religion, and "unique" historical events, we are developing an understanding of ecology, economy, and social structure, of behavioral modes, cultural continuity, and change.

The bulk of this new information has been got, not from the excavation of cemeteries or the re-examination of textual materials, but from the "problem-oriented" excavation of village sites. The value of such work was summarized by Adams[16] when he wrote that:

> . . . to dig graves is no more than to repeat the work which has been done again and again during the last half century. It reinforces the known without appreciably diminishing the un-

known. Yet profound gaps remain in the picture of Nubian and pre-Nubian culture history—particularly in regard to the periods of transition between one culture 'peak' and the next. Our best chance of learning something of these historical processes lies in the investigation of long-inhabited dwelling sites, where transition is spelled out by superposition.

The decision to excavate the Classic Christian Townsite at Arminna West was prompted by the hope of finding further stratigraphic evidence for continuity and change in Nubia and of clarifying parts of the typological system upon which much of Nubian culture history and chronology is based.

Between the villages of Derr and Toshka, the Nile Valley seems always to have been rich and fertile.[17] But to its south, from Toshka to Abu Simbel, the valley floor narrows, silt deposition diminishes, and the land is today, as it has been for millennia, among the poorest in all Nubia. It is in this barren stretch of rock and sand that the village we now call Arminna West was built.

The site of Arminna West lies directly across the river from the modern village of Arminna East, some four kilometers south of Toshka and twenty-six kilometers north of Abu Simbel, on the west bank of the Nile.[18] It covers an area approximately six hundred meters long and three hundred meters wide and lies in an area of wind-blown sand rising from *ca.* 119 to 126 m. above sea level. This area, called by Trigger the Plain of Arminna,[19] is typical of much of Lower Nubia (pl. I). The surface sand varies from a meter or more to only a few centimeters in depth and covers a bed of sandstone which continues west to a small series of hills a kilometer from the river. The cultivable land between the site and the river, which was flooded by the waters of the first Aswan Dam, probably was never more than a few decameters in width, although it becomes progressively wider as one approaches Toshka.

Arminna West may be divided into two large sections. Several hundred meters from the river, on a wide sandstone plateau, lies an extensive series of graves and pyramids (areas AWB and AWD), all of Meroitic and X-Group date.[20] Along the river, between two small patches of relatively arable land, lie the various portions of the Meroitic, X-Group, and Christian settlements. To the south, the areas labelled AWE and AWF represent houses and graves of the Late Meroitic period, while to the north, area AWK, the "Western Building," the "North Sector," and the Church represent periods of

11. Compare, for example, copies of such journals as *Antiquity* or *American Antiquity* between 1950 and 1965, or note the enormous number of books which set forth science for the archaeologist, most of which have appeared since 1960.

12. Two of the most important studies, both of which have greatly affected subsequent work, are J. G. D. Clark, *Prehistoric Europe, The Economic Basis* (London, 1951), and Gordon Willey, *Prehistoric Settlement Patterns in the Viru Valley, Bureau of American Ethnology, Bulletin 155* (Washington, D.C., 1953).

13. Adams, *JEA* 50 (1964); 51 (1965). See also his article in *Kush* X (1962): 245–88, and the discussion of Meroitic pottery in *Kush* XII (1964): 126–73.

14. Trigger, 1965.

15. Preliminary reports of Millet's excavations at Gebel Adda appear in *JARCE* III and IV. Gebel Adda is one of the few sites in Nubia to benefit from an application of pedological, biological, and zoological techniques. The final report should clarify many questions of ecology and culture in Nubia.

16. Adams, *Kush* X (1962): 17–18.

17. Trigger, 1965: 14.

18. UNESCO Survey, sheet 7, coordinates 699–700/975–976.

19. Trigger, 1967, pp. 1–2.

20. This portion of Arminna West is not yet published, but has been discussed by W. K. Simpson in several preliminary reports: see *Expedition* IV, 2 (1962); *Expedition* IV, 4 (1962); *Archaeology* XIV, 2 (1961); *Ventures* I (1962); and *Fouilles en Nubie* (1963).

Meroitic, X-Group, and Christian occupation. Portions of this northern area, particularly the "North Sector" and the Church, have recently been published by Bruce G. Trigger.[21] In the center of this eastern section, between area AWE and the Church and immediately adjacent to the river, lies the large complex of structures labelled the Classic Christian Townsite.

The history of archeological work at Arminna West has been summarized by Trigger,[22] who notes that most of the previous surveys and excavations have concentrated on the east bank of the river, near the modern village of Arminna East. Work was conducted here by Junker,[23] who excavated the cemetery Emery and Kirwan[24] labelled number 211, and the area has been briefly mentioned by several other investigators.[25] The only mention of the material at Arminna West, however, was made by Weigall in 1907,[26] by Monneret de Villard,[27] who thought the settlement to be a church, and by Junker in 1911. The last-named described the area thus:

> Eine Besichtigung des Westufers ergab
>
> 6) an der Südgrenze des Gebietes Ermenne in der Nähe der Niederlassung der Wüstenaraber in halber Höhe des Berges eine christliche Kirche und am Uferrand, zum grossen Teil vom Sande verschüttet, einen Komplex von Gebäuden der byzantinischen (christlichen) Epoche; es muss sich um eine ziemlich bedeutende Anlage handeln; der zu derselben gehörige Friedhof wird wohl dicht dabei unter dem Sande zu suchen sein, doch scheint auch auf halber Bergeshöhe ein Gräberfeld zu liegen.
>
> 7) Eine ähnliche Anlage sichteten wir weiter nördlich, ungefähr gegenüber der Landungsstelle von Ermenne.[28]

Trigger believes, and no doubt rightly so, that this reference is to the Classic Christian Townsite.[29]

The first intensive study of the Arminna West materials was conducted by the Pennsylvania-Yale Nubian Expedition in 1962–63. During the first season, work was begun in two small areas of the Townsite (areas A–U and C–U), but excavation was concentrated in the northern portion of the site where a Christian church and a series of Meroitic and Early Christian structures were uncovered.[30]

During this time, too, fairly extensive surface collections were made from the entire Plain of Arminna. In the autumn of 1963, excavations were resumed at the site. The first part of the season was devoted to an examination of a series of X-Group graves and Meroitic pyramids (area AWB) some 250 meters west of the Nile, and to a small series of Meroitic houses and Christian graves (areas AWE, AWF) at the southern limit of the site. The bulk of the season, however, was devoted to an excavation of the Classic Christian Townsite (see below, Part 2).

## II

In 1964 and 1965 two excellent syntheses of Nubian culture history appeared which dealt in considerable depth with the various problems of continuity and change in Lower Nubia during the last four millennia.[31] With these studies so readily available, and with a considerable amount of important comparative material as yet unpublished, it would be superfluous for us to attempt to trace the history and culture of Lower Nubia in these few pages. Instead, we propose briefly to discuss some problems related to Nubian culture-historical interpretation in terms of the data made available from excavations in the Arminna West Classic Christian Townsite.

In discussing archaeological interpretations of Nubian materials, Trigger[32] has called attention to "an unfortunate tendency to describe any rambling complex as a monastery, when in fact many of them were probably concentrated village sites." After our first season of excavation at Arminna West we, too, fell into this pattern,[33] only to revise our interpretation after work in 1963 clearly indicated that the site could be nothing but a large, concentrated settlement. Both the artifacts and the plan of the site confirmed that the Classic Christian remains were those of a townsite which had been inhabited for a considerable period of time, one which had grown by accretion in directions determined by economy, environment, and population pressures, rather than a complex built as a contemporaneous unit and following a definite "master plan." In general, the Townsite bears resemblance to such sites as Debeira West (R.8, Western Part),[34] Ikhmindi,[35] Kasanarti (5–X–32, Final Phase),[36] Tamit,[37] Gezira Dabarosa (6–G–6),[38] and to Meinarti (6–K–3, Unit Houses, Level 5).[39] A glance at the plans of

21. Trigger, 1967.
22. *Ibid.*
23. Junker, 1925.
24. Emery and Kirwan, 1935, esp. I: 413–16.
25. These are discussed in Trigger, 1967.
26. Weigall, 1907: 124.
27. Monneret de Villard, 1935–57: I: 129. "Già il Weigall segnalava all'estremità settentrionale del distretto di Ermenne sulla riva occidentale, una rovina in mattoni che gli sembrava essere un monastero copto. Questa rovina è chiamata sul luogo col nome di Ambinirā: io non ho potuto se non osservarla superficialmente, e credo sia una chiesa. Il complesso meriterebbe uno scavo completo."
28. Junker, 1925: 4.
29. Trigger, 1967: 2.
30. This northern material is the subject of Trigger's study, *ibid.*

31. Trigger, 1965; Adams, *JEA* 50 (1964); 51 (1965).
32. Trigger, 1965: 149.
33. This view is expressed by Monneret de Villard (cited above), and by Simpson, *ILN* 239 (1961): 94–95. See also Oates, *JEA* 49 (1963).
34. Shinnie, *Kush* XII (1964): especially fig. 3.
35. Monneret de Villard, 1935–57: I: 66–73, especially fig. 59.
36. Adams, *Kush* X (1962): 10–18, and fig. 1.
37. Monneret de Villard, 1935–57: I: 145, fig. 131.
38. Hewes, *Kush* XII (1964): fig. 11.
39. Adams, *Kush* X (1962): 10–18, fig. 3.

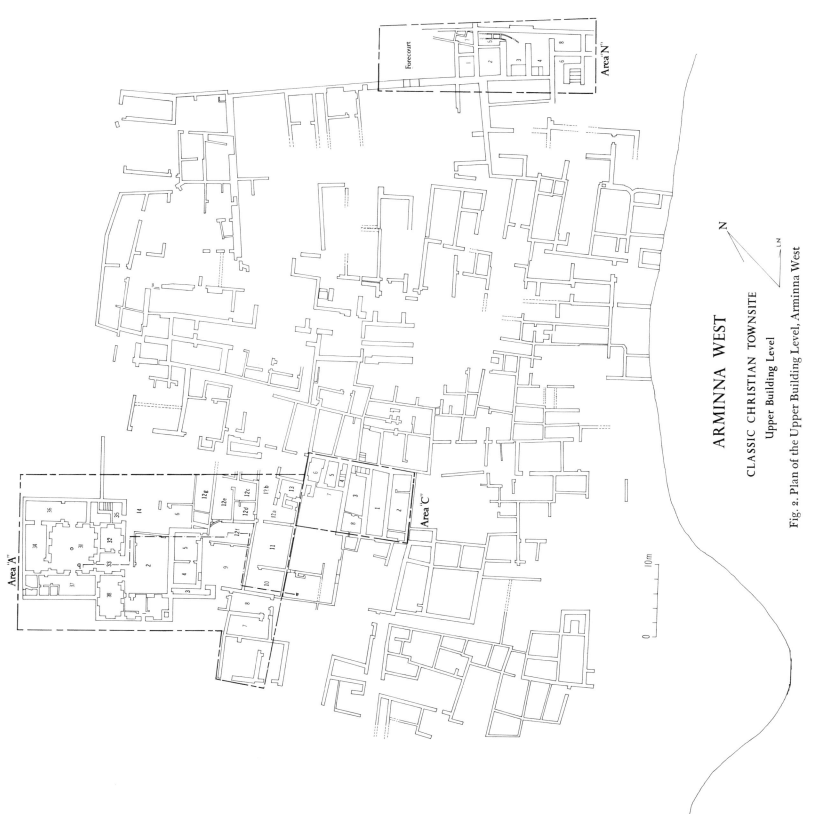

ARMINNA WEST

CLASSIC CHRISTIAN TOWNSITE

Upper Building Level

Fig. 2. Plan of the Upper Building Level, Arminna West

such monasteries as Ghazali,[40] Kasr el Wizz,[41] or Epiphanius,[42] will show the often marked differences between these two types of sites.

Between the two fortified towns and ceremonial centers of Kasr Ibrim and Gebel Adda, Trigger has noted the presence of twelve Late Nubian settlements, ranging in size from small dwelling sites such as Masmas to large complexes such as Arminna West.[43] Of these twelve sites, seven were apparently inhabited only during Christian times, one only during Meroitic times (Toshka), while four (Kasr Ibrim, Abu Simbel Town B, Gebel Adda, and Arminna West) gave evidence of occupation from Meroitic times until at least the twelfth to fourteenth centuries A.D. Since there is no evidence to suggest that Arminna West was a ceremonial or administrative center as were Kasr Ibrim or Gebel Adda, it must be assumed that this continuous occupation was due instead to a combination of economic and ecological factors which could at least minimally support its population. Thus, although from an historian's standpoint the Classic Christian Townsite may offer only slight interest, to the anthropologically oriented archaeologist it provides an important body of data for the study of sociocultural continuity and ecological adaptation.

In an earlier volume in this series, Trigger examined the Meroitic materials from Arminna West in considerable detail. The Meroitic remains in the Townsite (areas A–M and A–L) substantiate his conclusions but are not in themselves sufficient to merit another synthesis here. We shall therefore concentrate upon materials of the X-Group and Christian periods and refer the reader to the works of Trigger[44] and Adams[45] for summaries of Meroitic Lower Nubia.

The question of cultural continuity in Nubia is one which, until recent years, has been generally ignored. Most writers have tended to concentrate upon the differences between the Meroitic and X-Group or X-Group and Christian periods, although all of them have, of course, commented upon the similarities.[46] So strong are these similarities, in fact, that Adams[47] has remarked that, "earlier analyses to the contrary, it is the differences between the two and not the similarities which require explanation." Trigger[48] has described the X-Group period (his Ballana phase) as "essentially a continuation of the Meroitic," and both he and Adams have called attention to the lack of evidence for sudden change between Meroitic and X-Group times.[49] Between the two, as Trigger points out,[50] there was a period of transition which can be documented by ceramic change, architectural styles, genetic relationships, and the stratigraphic record. This period of transition apparently extended from the beginning of the third century A.D. until the middle of the fourth century.[51]

The transition from Meroitic to X-Group culture at Arminna West was apparently a gradual one,[52] and materials from area A–M of the Classic Christian Townsite indicate it was not brought about by conquest or invasion but rather by absorption and adoption. The buildings of this level, originally constructed during Late Meroitic times, were re-used during this later period and, in their lower strata, show a mixture of Late Meroitic and X-Group sherds which cannot be explained satisfactorily except by assuming that some Meroitic vessels were used during early X-Group times. There is also reason to believe that during X-Group times these structures functioned for the same purposes as they did during the Meroitic period. Although this is by no means a strong argument, it does lend support to the idea that the basis of X-Group society was generally similar to that of the preceding Meroitic period, i.e., with nuclear families occupying single dwellings.[53]

The degree of similarity between the X-Group and Christian periods has been more generally recognized than that between X-Group and Meroitic, but here again there has been a tendency to emphasize the differences, although these are generally in the sphere of religion.[54] The Christian period in Nubia has been divided by Adams[55] into three phases: Early, Classic, and Late. At Arminna West, the Early Christian phase is best represented by the northern portion of the Plain of Arminna and has been discussed by Trigger.[56] The Classic and Late Christian phases account for the bulk of the materials in the Townsite.

The Early Christian Phase, historically said to begin in A.D. 543 when missionaries of the Emperor Justinian

40. Shinnie and Chittick, 1961: fig. 2.

41. Briefly described in Smith, 1952.

42. Winlock, Crum, and White, 1926. Also of interest is Monneret de Villard, 1927, fig. 29.

43. Trigger, 1965, appendix 3. He lists Kasr Ibrim (fort and town), Masmas, Toshka, Arminna, Er Rammal, Tamit, Gindinarri, Abu Simbel North, Abu Simbel Town "A," Abu Simbel Town "B," and Gebel Adda.

44. Trigger, 1965 and 1967.

45. Adams, *Kush* XII (1964): 126–73, and *JEA* 50 (1964).

46. Adams, *Kush* XII (1964): 166.

47. Adams, *Kush* XII (1964): 163.

48. Trigger, 1965: 133, citing Junker, 1925: 85.

49. But cf. Emery, 1938, I: 22–23. Adams' site of Meinarti apparently offers a sound stratigraphic record of this continuity; Adams, *Kush* XII (1964): 163.

50. Trigger, 1965, 1967. Recent anthropological studies at Gebel Adda tend to confirm the idea of continuity in the population, but cf. Firth, *ASN* (1912): 36, and Reisner, *ASN* (1910): 345.

51. An extensive discussion of this period appears in Trigger, 1967. He notes that the idea is not new to the literature, and cites Emery and Kirwan, 1935: 70–105, and Reisner, *ASN* (1910): 149–55.

52. Again discussed by Trigger, 1967: 78 ff.

53. Adams and Nordström, *Kush* XI (1963), especially pp. 24–28.

54. Adams, *JEA* 51 (1965): 173.

55. Adams, *Kush* XII (1964): 216–48.

56. Trigger, 1967.

converted the inhabitants of Lower Nubia, lasted for about three centuries. It was a time when trade with Egypt was considerable but, at the same time, a period when indigenous developments and independence were asserting themselves. The use of vaults was revived after a decline during X-Group times, and some changes in ceramics can be seen, but, except for religion, little was different from the preceding phase. At Arminna West, Early Christian remains are found both in the "North Sector"[57] and in area "A–U" of the Townsite. These latter structures, which include a most impressive "Public Building," would appear to date from the beginning or middle of Early Christian times.[58] Trigger[59] comments that the smaller Early Christian towns were apparently rather poor, but judging from the structures in area A–U, this condition may not have been widespread or particularly severe.

The Classic Christian Phase, from about A.D. 850 to 1100, represents what some have described as the cultural zenith of Christian Nubia. Certainly Trigger[60] is correct when he states that it "reached heights unexcelled as far back as Meroitic times." It was a time of stability and prosperity, of a substantial trade with Egypt (during the last century of the phase), and of villages which formed tightly knit units and consisted of finely built houses. The Townsite at Arminna West is a fine example of this pattern. Houses (such as that in area C–U) were large, often with as many as eight or more rooms, were covered with carefully constructed barrel vaults, and were well-plastered. Despite their larger size, Adams[61] believes them to have been occupied by nuclear families and their clustering to reflect a highly integrated society rather than a concern for defense.

We have estimated that the population at Arminna West during this period was between 100 and 200 persons. Without a satisfactorily detailed ecological study of this area, we cannot, of course, say to what extent this population was dependent upon trade for its existence or to what degree its own agricultural pursuits satisfied dietary needs. But it would seem safe to state that, if this population was not large enough to require foodstuffs from more fertile areas near Toshka, it certainly would have been the maximum which its own lands could have supported.

If, as Adams suggests,[62] there was a flood during the ninth and tenth centuries which forced many Nubian peoples to move, there is little evidence of it at Arminna.

The population may have declined during this time, but the continuity of deposits and of material remains would suggest a life only little affected by such a rise. There is, for example, no evidence of a movement within the site to higher ground, although this can to some extent be accounted for by the original height of the village. Still, such a flood would have endangered the crops of the populace and, to explain a continued existence at what appears to be the same standard, one must assume either a trade in foodstuffs with areas relatively less affected by the rising waters or less of a dependence upon agriculture than has been supposed.

The Late Christian Phase (A.D. 1100 to 1300) was a period of rapid decline, particularly in Lower Nubia, where raids from Egypt and from the desert were most strongly felt. Kasr Ibrim was sacked in 1171 and the lands south to at least Adindan were pillaged.[63] Towns which continued in the area seem to have been concerned with defensive fortifications,[64] while trade declined to its lowest point in all Christian Nubian history. The Townsite at Arminna West was occupied at least during the first century of the Late Christian period, although the standard of living seems to have declined. It is interesting that, despite the twelfth-century invasions from the north, the subsequent pillaging of villages along the Nile, and the construction of defensive arrangements during this time, the Arminna West Townsite shows none of the presumed effects. It may be that by this time the village was considered unimportant and ignored or that the raids in the area were concerned only with obtaining foodstuffs and not with sacking. Yet it may well have been these raids which, indirectly, caused the abandonment of the Townsite sometime during the thirteenth or early fourteenth centuries A.D.

As we have already noted, trade was extremely important to the inhabitants of Nubia, both directly as a source of much-needed materials and indirectly as a cause of many of the invasions that helped mould its history. This trade was carried on from the beginnings of the Old Kingdom in Egypt (and even before) and lasted well into the present millennium. But, as Adams points out,[65] "at no time in Nubian history is the importance of trade more apparent than in the Christian period." For the archaeologist, evidence of this trade is of considerable concern, for its material remains and the texts relating to it have been one of the most important blocks upon which the chronological foundation of Nubian history has been constructed. Yet surprisingly enough, the nature of this trade is still only little understood.

During the Early Christian phase a fairly extensive trade seems to have been conducted with Egypt, and

57. *Ibid.*

58. See below, Part 2, chapter one, and Part 3, chapter one. Some important comments about the pottery of late Early Christian times appear in Adams, *Kush* XII (1964): 173.

59. Trigger, 1965: 146.

60. *Ibid.,* p. 147.

61. *Op. cit.,* p. 148.

62. Adams, *JEA* 51 (1965): 175; Adams and Nordström, *Kush* XI (1963): 42.

63. Arkell, 1961: 195; Trigger, 1965: 149; Adams, *JEA* 51 (1965): 175; Shinnie, 1954: 7; Monneret de Villard, 1938: 15–16.

64. Adams, *Kush* XII (1964): 231.

65. Adams, *JEA* 51 (1965): 176; Trigger, 1965: 166, table 6.

large numbers of wine amphorae have been found in literally every site of this phase. Adams[66] believes that the treaty made with Abdallah ibn Saad in 652 is indicative of its extent and importance, and it is interesting to note that the terms called for a payment of about 400 slaves in return for cloth, horses, and foodstuffs.[67] At Ikhmindi, the presence of a caravanserai may be indicative of its extent, both geographically and quantitatively.[68]

This extensive trade all but disappeared during the middle of the eighth century, at least in some fields, for trade wares became extremely scarce and remained so for over two hundred years. Adams[69] believes this to have been due in part to the overthrow of the Omayyad caliphate and to a sacking of Egyptian monasteries with which the extensive wine trade was conducted. There are several examples of the trade treaty being broken at this time, although Trigger suggests these may reflect the Nubians' attempt to better their bargaining position rather than a cessation of trade because of political affairs.[70]

Perhaps due to the Nubian occupation of Aswan, Egyptian trade goods again appeared in Nubia after A.D. 1000,[71] although this revival of economic relations seems to have been rather short-lived. As local manufacturing grew during Classic Christian times the need for imported goods decreased and, more important still, the desert routes between Egypt and the south were beginning to overshadow the former routes along the Nile in their importance, leaving Nubia more a spectator than a participant in Egyptian dealings with the Sudan.[72]

One of the problems in discussing the importance of trade during Christian times in Nubia is the tendency to treat it as a single, homogeneous entity. Although it is no doubt true that its various aspects were interrelated, it would nevertheless seem more meaningful to divide the trade into four categories:

(a) Nubian trade with Egyptian monasteries (wine), indicated by the presence of amphorae;
(b) Nubian trade with Egypt (foodstuffs, animals, cloth, etc.),

described in texts but often difficult to identify archaeologically;
(c) Nubian trade with the south (as indicated, e.g., by Adams' Ware Group III); and
(d) Local inter-village trade (difficult to identify archaeologically or textually).

The first two of these categories are the most frequently discussed in the literature and are generally treated together.[73] But, although they were both subject to many of the same political and economic problems, and were dependent upon the same methods of shipping, their origins are different and, presumably, the demand for them, at least on the village level, would have been subject to different pressures.

The trade with the south, archaeologically indicated by Adams' Ware Group III, and implicit in several texts, is largely a result of the Nubian–Egyptian trade, and it seems probable that the slaves given in exchange for Egyptian foodstuffs, cloth, and horses were obtained by trade (or perhaps to a small extent by raiding) in areas south of major Christian influence.[74]

It is highly unlikely that the trade with Egypt or the Sudan could have been conducted by individual settlements. Rather, one would suspect that certain large administrative centers served as headquarters for the trade, in a sense acting as agents for the district they represented. In Lower Nubia, Kasr Ibrim and Gebel Adda may well have served as such centers.

In addition to trade between these Nubian centers, Egypt, and the south, there was probably a fourth type, an exclusively inter-village trade. Some of this was no doubt conducted strictly between the settlements, without the larger towns acting as economic intermediaries. At Arminna West, for example, we have already suggested that the cultivable land may have been insufficient to support the Townsite population, at least in times of subnormal crops, and that additional wheat, barley, and other foodstuffs had to be acquired from areas of greater productivity. (Such an area in fact existed only a few kilometers away, near Toshka). Nicholas Millet[75] has suggested that the importance of herding activities in Nubian villages may be considerably underestimated. There is certainly evidence of such activity at Arminna West, particularly during the Classic and Late Christian phases (in area A–U and N–U), and it may well be that animals or hides were traded for foodstuffs at this inter-village level. Such a trade would have served as a most efficient means of equalizing the distribution of staples at an inter-village, intra-district level.

---

66. Adams, *Kush* X (1962): 280.

67. The treaty is cited by Arkell, 1961: 186–88, and is presented in detail by MacMichael, 1922: I, 157–58. Trigger, 1965 points out that these slaves were most probably not Lower Nubians but were obtained farther south.

68. Stenico, *Acme* XIII (1960): 47.

69. Adams, *Kush* X (1962): 280–81; *JEA* 51 (1965): 173–74; Arkell, 1961: 188–89.

70. Trigger, 1965: 148.

71. Adams, *JEA* 51 (1965): 175. Millet (1966: personal communication) reports finding several tombstones at Gebel Adda of the early 11th century belonging to Moslem traders. He believes their presence at Adda to be indicative of the extent and importance of this trade and to reflect the generally increased interest in the South during Fatimid times.

72. *Ibid.,* p. 177.

73. See, e.g., Arkell, 1961; Adams, *JEA* 50 (1964), 51 (1965); *Kush* X (1962): 281, ftn.; Trigger, 1965.

74. *Supra,* ftn. 67.

75. N. B. Millet (1966: personal communication). The author is deeply indebted to Mr. Millet for his suggestions regarding Part 1 of this report.

A second type of intra-Nubian trade would have existed between the trade centers such as Kasr Ibrim or Gebel Adda and the villages within their domain. By means of such relations, villages would have received the imported Egyptian goods, offering in exchange foodstuffs, animals, or hides. Some of these goods could then have been sent north in addition to the southern goods for which Nubia acted as intermediary, and others of them could have been stored or distributed to other villages, perhaps as trade goods, perhaps simply as dole.

If this series of conjectures is correct, the four types of trade in which Nubia participated could be diagrammed thus:

helped to clarify some of the questions posed by the materials at Arminna West.

Of particular interest in this regard are the frequencies of Adams' ware groups II, III, and V. Ware group II, for example, "Imported Egyptian Wares of the Early Christian Period," which is said to occur abundantly in Nubia and to suggest an extensive wine trade with Upper Egypt, is not particularly common at Arminna West. Its low frequency at a site so far north would seem to indicate either that Arminna West during Early Christian times was not a particularly wealthy settlement or that the trade between the village and the trade centers consisted of other commodities.[77] Of interest too is the presence of

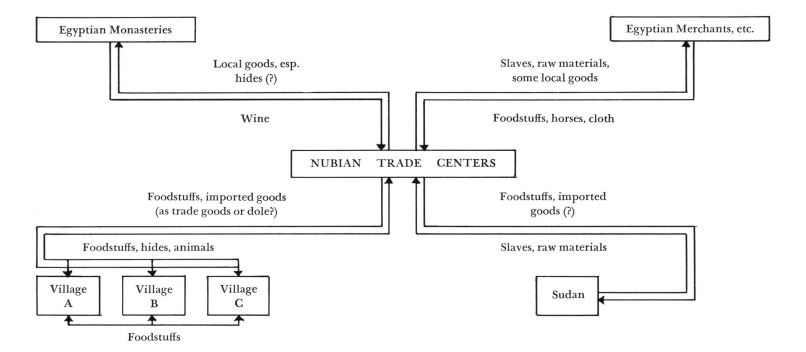

A major reason for the categorization of trade made above is that, at various levels, as shown on this chart, the economic relations assume a markedly different form. The trade between Egypt, the Sudan, and the Nubian trade centers would seem to be of a reciprocal type, while that between the trade centers and the villages is redistributive and that between the villages themselves utilizes a system of exchange.[76] However tenuous this picture may be, it does seem a useful model to follow in tracing the rise or decline of Egyptian trade with Nubia, and it has

ware group III, "Imported Southern (?) Wares of the Early Christian Period," which are said by Adams to have come perhaps from as far south as the Fourth Cataract,[78] and the complete absence of ware group V, "Imported Egyptian Wares of the Late Christian Period," a fact which would point either to the increasing isolation of Arminna West at least in the economic sphere, or to the site's impoverishment and decline. It is hoped that, after several of the recently excavated and particularly important sites in Lower Nubia have been published, a more detailed study of Christian Nubian economy can be pre-

76. The material on this trade is extremely scattered and of variable quality. The following sources were made use of in the preparation of this section: Trigger, 1965; Adams, *JEA* 50 (1964), 51 (1965), *Kush* X (1962): 245–88; Arkell, 1961; MacMichael, 1922; Butzer, *Bull. Soc. Geog. d'Egypte* 33 (1960); Kirwan, *LAAA* 24 (1937); Christophe, *Bull. Soc. Geog. d'Egypte* 35 (1963); Winlock, Crum, and White, 1926. See also: M. J. Herskovits, *Economic Anthropology* (New York: 1952) and Karl Polanyi, *et al., Trade and Market in the Early Empires* (New York: 1957).

77. If, as Millet and Adams suggest (1966: personal communications), the so-called gold-washing stations of Nubia are in fact connected with a local wine industry, then the absence of this ware group may be explained simply by the fact that there was no need to import a commodity which could be obtained locally (see also Trigger, 1965).

78. See below, Part 3, chapter two, section II.

pared. Until that time, the picture offered above must remain an unproved hypothesis, subject to considerable revision.

In the remainder of this report, we have tried to present a purely descriptive study of the materials from the Townsite at Arminna West, hoping that what now appear to be minor details may someday help shed light upon the sociocultural character of Lower Nubia. To this end, we have particularly concentrated upon the ceramic materials, for it is here that our knowledge of chronology and change is most rapidly developing. In sites such as the Arminna West Townsite, where texts and datable artifacts are extremely rare, the pottery provides almost the only key to such problems, and an understanding of geographical variation in form, style, and frequency becomes of critical importance. Despite the large numbers of texts from Nubian sites, reconstruction of the cultural history of Nubia during the Meroitic, X-Group, and Christian periods must depend heavily upon such archaeological material.

# PART 2

# ARCHITECTURE AND STRATIGRAPHY

*Chapter One:*

## Upper Building Level

WHAT WE HAVE TERMED the Upper Building Level of the Arminna West Classic Christian Townsite is an extensive area of structures, only a small portion of which is shown on the plan of the site (fig. 1). Scattered surface features, too small and vague to be mapped, show themselves all along the Plain of Arminna, and there are numerous indications that the village at one time curved in a gentle arc from area "A," behind the Church, east toward the cultivation several hundred meters to the north.[1]

During the 1962 season, a small series of rooms near the southern end of the Townsite was cleared and planned. This area, which consisted of eight rooms (area C–U), gave evidence that the larger and better-preserved structures in the Townsite were filled almost exclusively with wind-blown sand. Although these rooms were of architectural interest, it became clear that an understanding of the area would require data which could only be got from stratified materials. Surface surveys and a small sondage showed that such material could only be found at the edges of the building complex and, consequently, during the 1963 field season, it was decided to restrict excavation to the Townsite's northern and southern limits.

To the north, a series of eight rooms built against a major east-west wall of the site, and lying *ca.* 80 m. south of the Classic Christian church,[2] was excavated to the lower levels of the Upper Building. The area has been labelled "N–U" and is described in detail below.

To the south, excavations in 1962 had been conducted in area C–U and in the southwest corner of the Townsite in what was later termed the Public Building, the latter considered here as a portion of area A–U. These two areas lay roughly on the sides of a large rectangle and it seemed useful to conduct a more extensive excavation between them, tying them together stratigraphically and architec-

turally, providing a large area within which building plan and sequence could be studied. This large area has been labelled area "A," and excavations here were carried down through three major building levels (A–U, A–M, and A–L) until ground water prevented further work.

In this chapter we shall describe in detail the rooms of these various areas (A–U, C–U, and N–U). In Chapter Two we shall offer a discussion of the Middle Building level (A–M) and of the lowest levels of the excavation (A–L).

## I: Area "A–U"

The excavation unit designated as area "A" measured *ca.* twenty-five meters in width (north to south) and thirty-eight meters in length, including within it an extensive series of houses and other structures (rooms 2–14) and a complex of rooms known as the Public Building (rooms 1, 31–39). The Public Building had been cleared during the 1962 season and in 1963 we used it as the starting point for excavation. A small collection of surface sherds was made, and the first fifty to seventy-five centimeters of sand removed from the entire area, thus exposing the tops of most of the walls. All materials from this first stripping operation have been labelled as surface finds because of the great degree to which the material had been disturbed. References to finds from "level 1," therefore, exclude this surface material, and in most cases begin at the top of the walls in any given room (pls. II, III, IV, V).

### *Individual Room Descriptions*

#### *Room A–U–2*

This room, which measured *ca.* 5.80 x 8.50 m., is of interest both because of its location immediately adjacent to the Public Building and its position directly above the excavated portion of the Middle Building level.

Level 1, which extended from the top of the walls to an average depth of 126.45 m. above sea level, consisted exclusively of wind-blown sand with a few mixed sherds. Floor I, directly below this level, was of compacted silt and mud, varying in elevation from 126.35 to 126.65 m. Directly on the floor, against the east wall, lay a small platform of mud and mud brick measuring 60 x 40 x 8 cm., presumably used as a pottery stand or as the base of a storage bin.

The foundation of the screen wall at the north and west ends of the room lay at an average of 126.60 m., directly on the surface of floor I. It was built of a single row of mud bricks and had three small pylons at the north, south, and east ends bonded to it for additional support. Both surfaces of the wall were covered with a layer of mud plaster *ca.* 2 cm. thick. Floor I ran beneath this wall to the walls of A–U–31 and A–U–32 where it broke off,

---

1. The northern portion of the Plain of Arminna is discussed in detail by Trigger, 1967.

2. For a description of the latter structure see Trigger, 1967.

apparently having been destroyed by the construction of the Public Building.

Floor I may be equated with the first floor levels of rooms A–U–4 and A–U–5 and was contemporaneous with the construction of the room 3–4–5 unit (pl. IIe). At the south end, the wall of room A–U–1 lay slightly above floor I, at an elevation near that of the north screen wall. The latter is probably contemporaneous with, or only slightly later than, the Public Building complex.

Beneath floor I was a layer of compact sand (level 2) which extended down to the walls of the Middle Building. The numerous sherds of this second stratum were generally of Classic Christian date.

### Room A–U–3 (fig. 3)

Measuring 5.00 x 0.80 m., room 3 was filled with almost one meter of dirt, ash, and burnt sherds. At 126.40 m. this changed to a layer of fine silt, but there was no indication of any floor or occupation level. The room was covered by a low barrel vault and the foundations of the walls lay at an average depth of 126.40 m., the resulting low ceiling making it highly doubtful that the room could have functioned as a chamber for habitation or for storage. One is more inclined to believe that it served as a foundation for some structure above. The ash deposit within the room would indicate that the materials were dumped here after the second story (if there were such) and the vault had been destroyed. This ash most closely resembles that found associated with various ovens in the site both in composition and consistency, and probably came from such a source (perhaps from the oven in A–U–6) rather than from any razed structure.

The heavy, well-built walls of the room have provided an important clue for determining the building sequence of the Townsite, for they clearly show that rooms 3, 4, and 5 formed a single contemporaneous unit which pre-dated the construction of the Public Building. A heavy layer (ca. 3–4 cm. thick) of well-made mud plaster covered the walls of the unit and separated the walls of A–U–1 and A–U–3.

Sherds from the ash layer were numerous and quite amorphous, ranging from Early Christian to Late Christian times.

### Rooms A–U–4 and A–U–5 (fig. 3; pl. IIb, d)

The architectural unit formed by rooms 3, 4, and 5 is one of the most clearly defined and well-constructed parts of the Upper Building level. As noted above, these rooms shared common walls, ca. 70 cm. thick, covered with a heavy layer of well-made mud plaster which contained large quantities of straw and chaff. They can be definitely shown to pre-date the Public Building. There is reason to believe that this unit was the first to be constructed in area "A–U," and one of the first in the Upper Building generally.

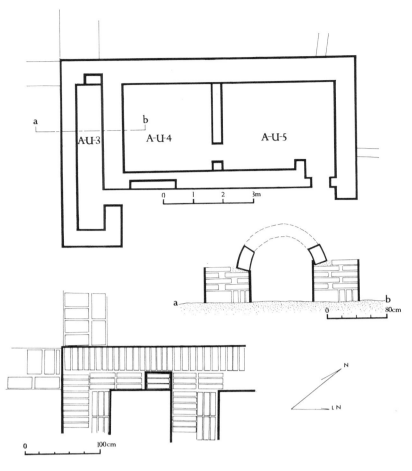

Detail of SW Corner, A–U–3

Fig. 3. Plan and architectural details of rooms A–U–3, 4, 5

Rooms 4 and 5 were joined by a doorway through a wall built after the main walls of the rooms were completed. There were no indications of a sill. The floor between rooms 5 and 12f did have a stone sill, however, slightly out of place when found, with no hinge-stone. Both doorways were 50 cm. wide.

The construction of the outside walls indicates that the rooms were vaulted, and since the foundation of the secondary wall between them lay at the same elevation as the main walls (126.40 m.), it seems likely that it was built as much to provide additional structural support as to divide the interior area. This secondary wall, which was 40 cm. thick, was not plastered, but in brick size and method of construction was the same as the major walls of the room (pl. IId). Room 4 was almost exactly three meters square and room 5 was 3.00 x 3.75 m.

The level of floor I in both rooms lay at an average of 126.42 m. and consisted of a heavy layer of well-compacted silt and mud. There were no features associated with it. In level 2, the situation was identical to that in room 2, where a thick layer of compact sand extended down to the walls of the Middle Building.

The pottery from both levels 1 and 2 must be assigned an Early Christian date. Indeed, that from level 2 may also be Transitional or X-Group.

*Room A–U–6 (fig. 4; pl. IIIb, e)*

Measuring 3.00 m. wide and 3.20 m. long, the room was formed by a small wall (*ca.* 20 cm. thick) on its north and east sides which abutted the north wall of room 5. The foundations of this wall lay at 126.12 m. The west side of the room was formed by a wide doorway.

Beneath a layer of wind-blown sand, a thin floor of well-compacted silt and mud was found extending over a portion of the room at an average of 127.25 m. On this floor, in the northeast corner of the room, was a thick deposit of almost pure ash on top of which several mud bricks had been placed in irregular fashion. Against the south wall was a small, badly broken oven (pl. IIIe) containing ash and an occasional small sherd, and to its east, between the oven and the east wall, was a small workbench, *ca.* 25 cm. high and 30 cm. long, built of mud and mud brick.

Under floor I was a thick and extremely well-compacted layer of almost pure ash containing only traces of silt and organic material. Beneath this, at 126.88 m., was a second floor of compacted mud. At the west end of this floor was a small mud brick structure, a low platform which perhaps served as a foundation for a storage bin or for some type of work space. The oven noted above had its foundations within floor II and was probably contemporaneous with it. The adjacent bench, however, is to be associated with floor I.

Floor II lay at the same level as the first floor of room 14, and the two were joined by a wide (2.00 m.) doorway, at the south side of which lay a large hinge stone with its top *ca.* 5 cm. above the level of the floor. Against the north jamb was a smaller flat stone, perhaps a remnant of the door-sill.

Floor III, at 126.75 m., consisted of a thin layer of silt and well-compacted mud similar in composition to that of floors I and II, and ran well under the small pit dug to accommodate the oven. A small screen wall, which first appeared in level 2, lay in the center of the doorway and was contemporaneous with floor III.

Beneath floor III, in level 4, was a thick layer of light brown soil, a thin layer of silt and clay, and a layer of sand which extended into the upper portion of the Middle Building (fig. 4; pl. IIIe).

Sherds from the upper strata were of Late Christian times. Those of level 3 can be assigned a Classic Christian date, and those of level 4, although scarce, are apparently of Early Christian times.

*Room A–U–7*

The room was cleared of sand, but time did not permit its complete excavation. According to the architect's report, the technique of construction, the brick size, and the foundation level (tested in one corner of the room), are sufficiently similar to those of the room 3–4–5 unit to

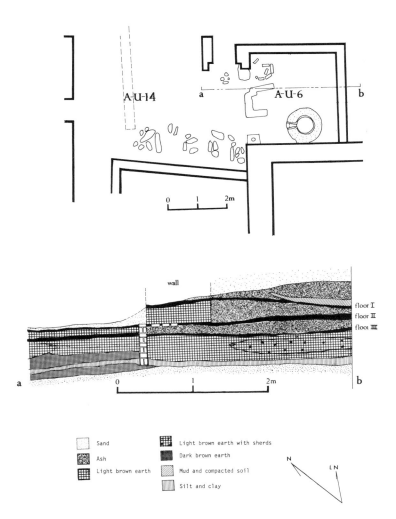

Fig. 4. Plan and stratigraphic profile of rooms A–U–6, 14

suggest that the two are contemporaneous. The sherds from the sand layer would confirm this date.

*Room A–U–8*

Beneath a layer of wind-blown sand, floor I lay at 126.45 m. No features were associated with the floor, and sherds from the level above it were extremely scarce. Examination of the room's north, east, and west walls showed them to be of more recent date than those of room 7. From the foundation levels (126.38 m. for the north wall), and from the method of construction, room 8 may be equated with the east walls of rooms 10 and 11 (east wall foundation: 126.37 m.). The floor level was slightly lower than in adjacent rooms.

A large sealed jar containing the skeleton of a new-born child wrapped in coarse linen, and doubtless of fairly recent date, was found immediately above the floor in the northwest corner of the room.

*Room A–U–9 (pl. XIe)*

At an average of 126.50 m. a thin occupation level of compacted earth was found beneath a deep layer of wind-blown sand. Sherds from the level above floor I were relatively scarce and formed an amorphous collection. There were no associated features.

The foundation of the wall separating rooms 9 and 12f, a 25 cm. thick screen wall which abutted the west wall of room 11, lay at an average of 126.36 m. and was associated with floor III of room 12f, thus preceding floor I of room 9. Floor I would also seem slightly earlier than the wall between rooms 8 and 9. Thus, it would precede the construction of the upper walls to its east and southeast and would follow construction of the walls to its north and west.

Beneath floor I was a thick layer of compact sand which extended down to the tops of the walls in the Middle Building. From this stratum, sherds were of Early and Classic Christian date.

### Rooms A–U–10 and A–U–11 (fig. 5; pl. IIIc)

As we noted in describing room A–U–8, the east and south walls of room 10 were apparently contemporaneous and of an earlier date than the north and west walls. The floor of room 10, at 126.50 m., was composed of compact silt and mud and contained no features. It lay slightly above the foundations of the south, east, and west walls and at almost the same elevation as the north secondary wall. Sherds from level 1, above this floor, were of Classic and Late Christian date. Beneath floor I was a layer of compact sand which continued below the limit of excavation at 125.75 m. The doorway in the south wall of the room, 80 cm. in width, had a low sill of plastered mud brick which was quite well-preserved. Access to room 11 was gained by a 1.00 m. wide doorway at the west end of the 30 cm. thick secondary wall.

Floor I of room 11 lay at *ca.* 126.80 m. and had no associated features. Beneath it was a thin deposit of compact sand and silt, followed at 126.65 m. by floor II, again composed of mud and silt. This second floor, which was contemporaneous with floor I of room 10 and with the east-west cross wall separating the two rooms, at one time apparently extended into room 12a, but was broken and removed prior to the construction of the east-west cross wall separating rooms 11 and 12a. The foundation of this wall was at 126.76 m. at its eastern end, 126.96 m. at its western. Floor I of room 10 appears to have been contemporaneous with it. The foundation of the wall was built to take advantage of an extension of the wall between rooms 12d and 12f and of a somewhat later addition to this room 12 structure (fig. 7). This same technique was used in the construction of the northern portion of the western wall of rooms 10 and 11, which in part was built directly upon a wall extension lying east of room 12f.

On floor II, the badly broken remains of a small series of curtain walls lay in the northwest corner, adjacent to

the remains of an oven apparently of similar size and design to that in room A–U–6.

Between floors I and II, in level 2, sherds were of Classic Christian date, although some sherds of earlier periods were recovered from the area adjacent to the oven.

Architectural features point to the fact that rooms 10 and 11 were built after construction of the room 12 complex.

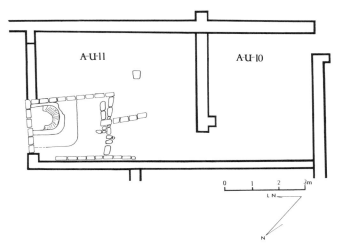

Fig. 5. Plan of rooms A–U–10, 11

### Rooms A–U–12a through A–U–12h (pl. XIh)

Beneath a layer of wind-blown sand, floor I of the room 12 complex lay in most cases above the level of the walls which later forced its sub-division into rooms "a" through "h." The elevation of floor I varied considerably, at the east end being *ca.* 127.10 m., at the west 127.33 m. The compact silts and mud which formed the floor, however, were consistent throughout the entire area.

Against the west wall of room 12b, which was visible at this level, lay three small circles of stone, probably used as supports for pottery vessels. There were no other features.

Beneath level 1 and floor I, the various cross walls were clearly visible and the A–U–12 area was therefore sub-divided into smaller rooms, each of which shall be dealt with separately. Level 2 consisted of compact sand, some silt and light gray ash, and extended from beneath floor I to the surface of floor II.

### Room A–U–12a (figs. 6, 7)

Floor II at 126.55 m. was of compact silt and mud and had no associated features. Beneath it was a heavy layer (level 3) of compact sand containing small quantities of ash and silt. Fragments of whitewashed mud plaster were found in the southern portion of the room and had probably fallen from the wall now underlying the east-west

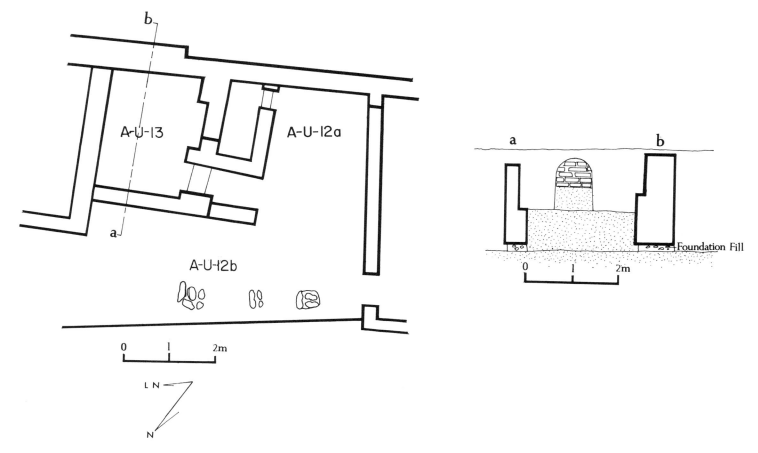

Fig. 6. Plan of rooms A–U–12a, 12b, and 13

cross wall between rooms 11 and 12a. In the northeast corner, directly on the floor, was a heavy deposit of ash, charcoal, and rock, presumably dumped here after the room had been abandoned. Floor II ran under the east wall of the room and, to the west, continued through room 12b to abut the wall between rooms 12b and 12d. A third floor, at 126.08 m., appeared to be contemporaneous with this western wall.

*Room A–U–12b* (fig. 6)

Stratigraphically, 12b was similar to room 12a. The level of floor II varied in elevation from 126.65 m. at the north end to 126.50 m. at the south, where it continued into room 12a. Floor III lay at 126.08 m. and appeared to be contemporaneous with the wall between 12b and 12c–d. The wall between it and room 13 lay slightly above the third floor, at 126.22 m.

Sherds from levels 1, 2, and 3 of both rooms 12a and 12b were of Late Classic Christian and Late Christian date. Those from level 4, beneath floor III, are of Early Christian times.

*Room A–U–12c* (fig. 8)

At one time a single large room, the construction of a 20 cm. thick wall formed two smaller rooms which we have

labelled 12c (*ca.* 2.80 x 2.50 m.) and 12d (2.50 x 2.75 m.). This cross wall, which lay at 126.25 m., was appreciably higher than the foundations of the east or west walls, both of which averaged 126.08 m. above sea level. On the floor of 12c (floor II, at 126.55 m.), in the northeast corner of the room, was a small oven of design similar to that in room 6 and perhaps similar to that in room 11. No other features were encountered and excavation of the room was halted at *ca.* 126.00 m.

Sherds from the upper level of the room were of Late Christian date; those between floors I and II were of Classic Christian times; and those within and beneath the lower floor were Early Classic Christian.

*Room A–U–12d* (figs. 8, 9)

On floor II, at 126.50 m., a low bench of mud brick ran adjacent to the north wall of the room and was formed in part by the upper courses of a wall of the Middle Building. A doorway at the south end of the east wall, which at one time gave access to room 12b, was subsequently blocked, and a thick block of ash and silt, covered with a single layer of mud brick, placed in front of the door. This blocking must have occurred shortly after the room was first used, and the mud and ash gives the impression of it having been a workspace associated with the ovens nearby.

14

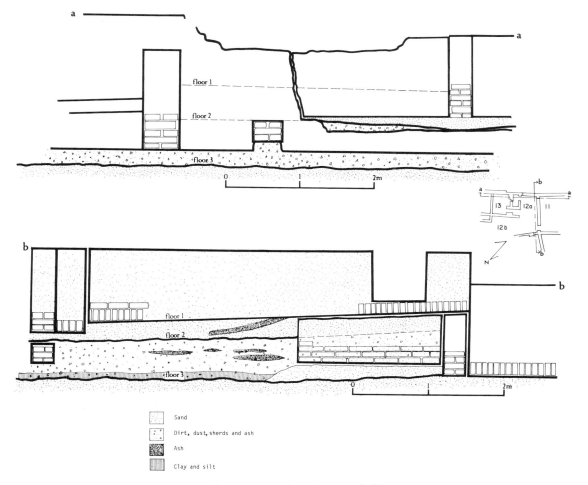

Fig. 7. Architectural sections of rooms A–U–12a, 13

The south and east walls of this room lay well below the walls of room 11 and served as their foundation. In the same way, the north wall of 12d was built directly upon the remains of a large mud brick wall of the Middle Building level.

Sherds from levels 1, 2, and 3 are of Classic and Late Christian date; those of level 4 are of the Early Christian period.

### Room A–U–12e (fig. 8)

Floor II, of compact silt and mud, lay at an average depth of 126.45 m. Floor III lay at 126.29 m. and in it, in the northeast corner of the room, were two stone circles probably used as pottery supports, and a large red-ware bowl.

Below floor III was a level of sand, ash, and silt with a small concentration of stone at the southern end of the room. The south and west walls of the room lay directly upon the tops of walls of the Middle Building level, as was the case in room 12d. Architectural materials would indicate, however, that 12e was built after both 12c and 12d. The room measures 5.30 x 2.50 m.

Sherds from all levels of the room are of late Classic and Late Christian times.

### Room A–U–12f (fig. 9)

Width at east end: 3.20 m.; at west end: 2.50 m.; length: 5.60 m. Floor II was again of compact silt and mud and lay at a depth of 126.87 m. On it was a fifteen centimeter high mud brick platform built against the southern wall of the room. At the west end of the room the floor was covered by a small deposit of dust and dirt, ca. 15 cm. thick, and, above this, a 10 cm. deposit of pure ash. There were no other features associated with the floor, and pottery from levels 1 and 2 was of Late Christian date.

Floor III lay at 126.28 m., and two small walls, presumably remnants of small platforms, lay at the room's eastern end, while a third ran from north to south through the middle of the room.

Beneath floor III, in level 4, sherds were of the Classic Christian period. The level consisted of wind-blown sand with occasional lenses of dirt and ash.

### Room A–U–12g

Floor II, lying at ca. 126.60 m., was of the usual silt-mud combination. At the room's northern end were two small circular pits, ca. 20 cm. deep, presumably used as pottery supports. The room was cut at the southern end by a small

15

cross wall, 20 cm. wide and now only two courses high, running east to west. The southern wall of the room was the heavy wall of A–U–5, and to its north was a small but equally well-constructed wall with an almost identical foundation level (126.45 m. as opposed to 126.50 m.). The wall, which ran at a slight angle ENE to WSW, extended below room 6 and room 12f. The room measured 2.20 m. in width and was 8.00 m. long.

### "Room" A–U–12h

Stratum 1 (of wind-blown sand) was removed but the room was not excavated.

### Room A–U–13 (figs. 6, 7; pl. IIc)

Level 1, extending to a depth of 126.90 m., was of wind-blown sand. Beneath it lay floor I, apparently contemporaneous with floor I of the 12a–h complex. It was at this level that the springers of the vault were found. Beneath floor I was a layer of sand and dirt. Floor II lay at 126.70 m. and, like floor I, lacked any features, but was a distinct occupation level of compacted silt and mud. Beneath this was a thick layer of dust, ash, and dirt. The third floor level of room 12a seems to have continued through this room. A low sill of mud brick in the door of the south

wall separated the room at this level from 12a. The foundations of the east, west, and south walls of the room were contemporaneous and all lay at 126.20 m. The low archway through the north wall opened onto floor II of the room. The addition of other walls at the south entrance effectively narrowed that doorway from 1.60 to 0.60 m. and were built prior to the use of floor II of room 12a, but after abandonment of floor III. The room measured *ca.* 2.80 x 2.50 m. Sherds were of Late Christian date.

Room 13 is an important element of the excavated portion of the site for it has provided one of the keys to building sequence in the southern portion of the Townsite and has allowed the architectural correlation of areas A–U and C–U.

### Room A–U–14 (fig. 4; pl. IIc)

Floor I of the room lay at an average of 126.87 m. It was contemporaneous with, and perhaps an extension of, floor II in A–U–6. A small circle of stones, adjacent to the entrance of room 6, was the only feature found.

Beneath floor I was a thin layer of sand, ash, and dirt which covered floor II at 126.62 m. Numerous large stones, together with a few mud bricks, lay in the southern portion of the room. Floor II was contemporaneous with floor III of A–U–6.

Sherds appear to have been of Classic Christian times.

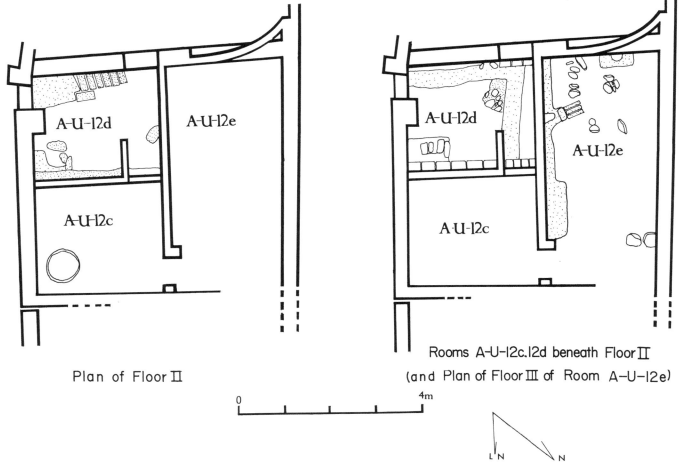

Plan of Floor II

Rooms A–U–12c.12d beneath Floor II
(and Plan of Floor III of Room A–U–12e)

0                                    4m

Fig. 8. Plans of floors II and III, rooms A–U–12c, 12d, 12e

*Rooms 1, 31–39: The Public Building*
(figs. 10–12; pls. IV, V)

That portion of area A–U which has been termed the Public Building consisted of a series of rooms which together formed a carefully designed, well-integrated, and solidly constructed unit. The floors were in places of flagstone paving, of mud brick, or of well-compacted silt and mud, and the walls were thick, carefully laid, heavily plastered, and at one time were whitewashed or perhaps painted.

The function served by this rather elaborate structure remains unknown. In some of its general characteristics it bears a similarity to several churches in the Lower Nubian area (e.g., Ar-Rammal and Serra),[3] while in others it vaguely resembles a simplified version of a castle or palace such as that at Karanog.[4] Neither of these,

3. Monneret de Villard, 1935–57: I: 203.
4. *Ibid.,* I: 105 for plan; and, of course, see Woolley, 1911.

however, church or castle, seem satisfactory explanations. Indeed, the general appearance of the unit is equally reminiscent of contemporary Nubian houses as of these earlier structures. To have served as a church, the building would have had to undergo numerous changes in design and construction, and there is no indication that such changes took place. To interpret the complex as a palace or castle would require substantiation from other evidence, both from texts and from artifacts, neither of which can be found. To call the building a house would also require additional data, for none of the usual accoutrements were present, and the care lavished on such details as the column in room 31 does not seem in keeping with such a function. Until such time as further comparative material becomes available, therefore, we have chosen to call this unit the "Public Building," hoping to convey by this term something of the quality and character of the construction without committing ourselves to the specific interpretations of function implicit

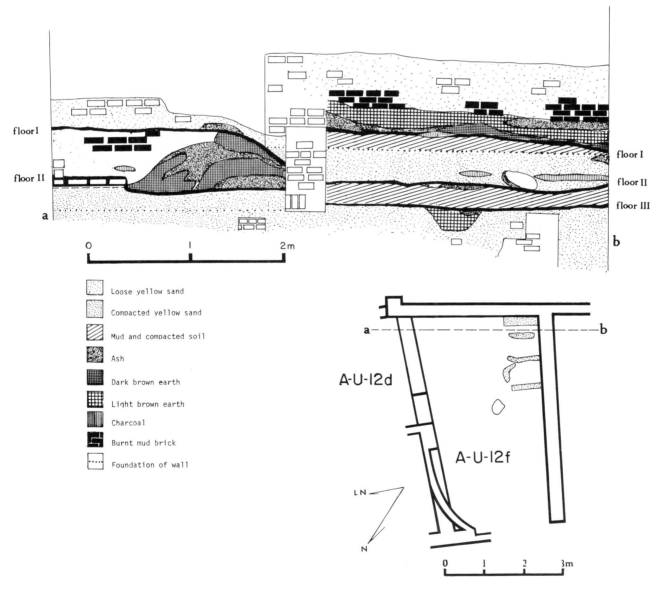

floor I

floor II

floor I
floor II
floor III

a

b

0        1        2 m

Loose yellow sand

Compacted yellow sand

Mud and compacted soil

Ash

Dark brown earth

Light brown earth

Charcoal

Burnt mud brick

Foundation of wall

A-U-12d

A-U-12f

LN

N

0    1    2    3m

Fig. 9. Stratigraphic profile and plan of rooms A–U–12d, 12f

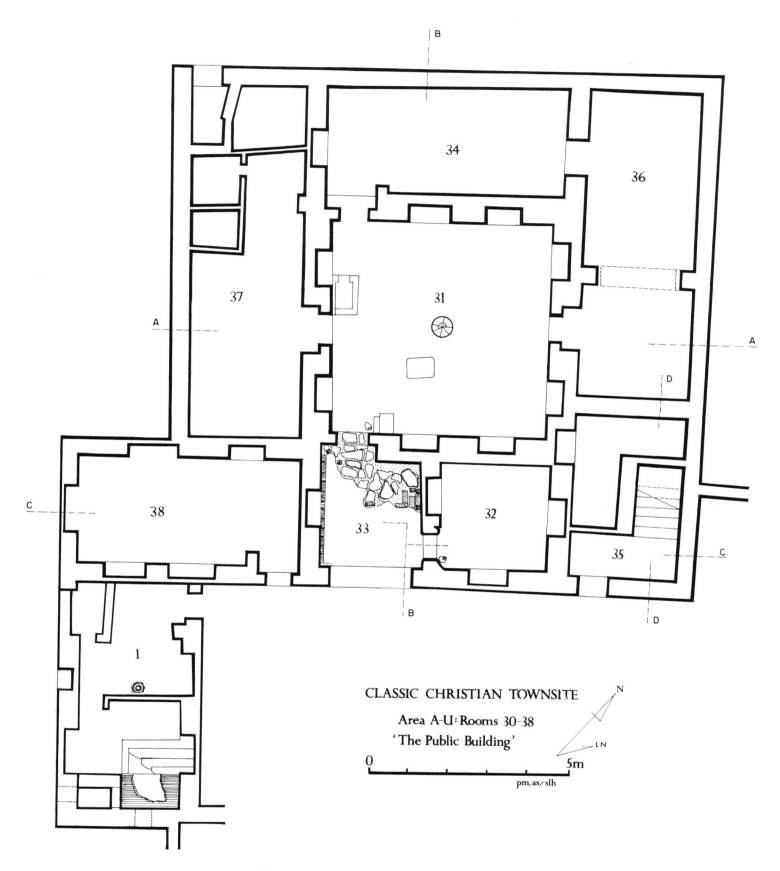

CLASSIC CHRISTIAN TOWNSITE

Area A-U: Rooms 30-38

'The Public Building'

0                                                                    5m

pm, as/slh

Fig. 10. Plan of "The Public Building," rooms 1, 30–38

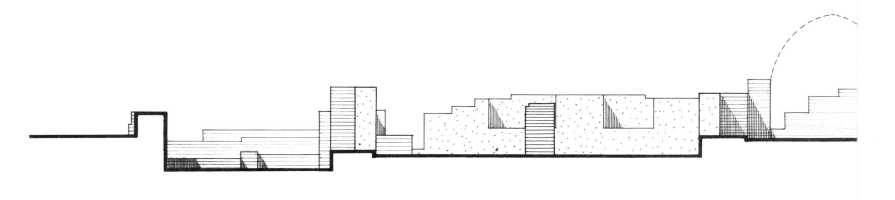

Section A-A

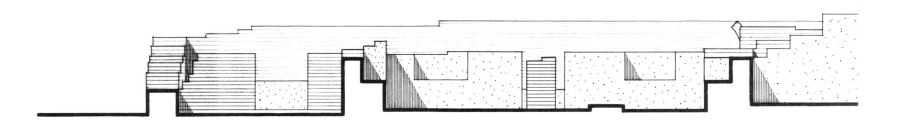

Section B-B

SITE

5m

in most other titles. In section IV of this chapter we shall again examine this problem.

Entrance to the Public Building was gained by a foyer (room 33) measuring *ca.* 2.50 x 3.00 m.[5] The floor of the room was paved with flagstone, laid down on a foundation of mud brick (pl. IVc). In the south wall was a niche 90 cm. wide and 50 cm. deep, similar to those found in rooms 31, 32, and 38. In no case could the height of these niches be determined because of the destruction of the upper part of the walls. The main entrance to the room was 2.00 m. in width, while that leading to room 32 was only 60 cm. (pl. Vb).

Room 32, measuring *ca.* 2.65 x 2.75 m., was paved with mud bricks and had three niches similar to those in rooms 31, 33, and 38. A small, irregular hinge stone was found in the southeast corner of the room adjacent to the door. There were no other features.

The largest room of the Public Building was room 31, measuring 5.55 x 5.55 m. Its floor was paved with mud, and 75 cm. wide doorways in its north, south, east, and west walls gave access to similarly paved floors in rooms 33, 34, 36, and 37. In each of its four walls were niches, 90 cm. wide and 50 cm. deep, all constructed so as to directly face those on opposing walls. Those in the north and south walls were separated by doorways. On the floor adjacent to the south wall of the room was a small mud brick structure, perhaps a platform of sorts, and adjacent to the east wall was another small platform or "wall" of mud brick. Both of these may be later additions to the room. The floor of this room lay at *ca.* 126.60 m., and above it were three strata: from the surface of the site to *ca.* 127.20 m. was wind-blown sand; from 127.20 to 126.95 m. was a mixture of silt, organic material, broken brick, and some sand; from 126.95 m. to the floor was heavily compacted sand.

All of the walls in the Public Building, including the interior of the niches, were covered with a heavy coat of fine mud plaster and were whitewashed.

The most interesting feature of room 31 was a mud brick column found almost exactly in the center of the room (pl. IVa, e). Having a diameter of 50 cm., it was preserved to a height of 14 courses, and was built on a foundation of sand laid down on the mud floor. The bricks (fig. 12) were of three forms: wedges, measuring 24.5 x 17.5 x 6.0 cm.; curved rim pieces, 34.5 (exterior) x 17.5 (interior) x 12.5 x 6.0 cm.; and circular fillers, 26 x 6 cm. The bricks were laid in alternate courses of wedges and curved rim pieces, the lower five rim courses having circular fillers to provide additional strength, the upper rim courses being filled with mortar. All of the

5. The description of the Public Building upon which this section is based is taken from the field notes of N. B. Millet, B. G. Trigger, and Peter Mayer, who conducted the clearing of the structure during the 1962 field season.

bricks were well-fired, and on each of them was a symbol, written with whitewash on the top surface. Some of these symbols can be recognized as Coptic letters or numbers; others of them, however, seem to have no parallel in published materials to which the writer had access. All of the bricks in any particular course were similarly marked, e.g., all four curved rim pieces in the 13th course had what appears to be the letter *rho* on them (or is it the number 100 or 900?); all eight wedges in the 8th course had what appears to be an *omega* (or is it the number 800?). During the summer of 1963 villagers or children destroyed this column and hence there is no record of the sequence in which these letters or numbers occurred. We may assume from the above two examples that it was not alphabetical or numerical.

The characters on each of these bricks were painted after the bricks had been baked (they were not fired), and one wonders if they might not have been put there to facilitate *re-erection* of the column rather than its original construction. For all intents and purposes, any variation in the size and shape of the individual bricks were extremely slight, never more than a millimeter or two, and such careful labelling of each piece would have been unnecessary for the construction of the column. It would seem that there were other than purely structural reasons for such markings.

When the Public Building was excavated there were no remnants of fallen walls lying in the fill. This rubble having been cleared away, perhaps during Classic or Late Christian times, there is no way to tell what the original height of the column in room 31 might have been. One cannot but feel, however, since it would have been structurally unable to support any vaulting or dome over the area, that it may well have stood no more than its present fourteen courses high, and perhaps served as a stand for some sort of table. A worked piece of stone lying near the column, measuring 70 x 55 cm., might have served as the top of such a feature.

Room 34 lay to the west of room 31 and was connected to it by a 75 cm. wide doorway. It measured *ca.* 6.10 x 2.75 m. and had one niche in its south wall. Fill in this room, as in all rooms of the Public Building, was similar to that in room 31. Its floor lay at 126.55 m., 5 cm. lower than that of room 31. There were no features.

Room 36 was joined to room 31 by means of a 75 cm. doorway and to room 34 by an 80 cm. passage. Its floor lay at *ca.* 126.70 m. Originally measuring 8.00 x 2.75, it was cut by the addition of a heavy mud brick wall to form two rooms, 4.60 m. and 2.75 m. in length, respectively. There were no features.

Room 35 is a small landing and stairwell for the staircase leading to either the roof or the second story of the Public Building. Access to the stairs was gained by a 70 cm. wide opening leading from the yard east of the Building. We assume that there were two flights of stairs,

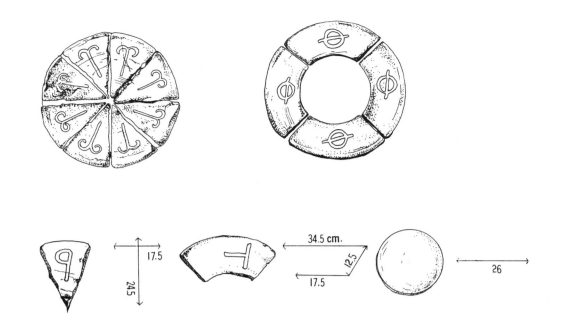

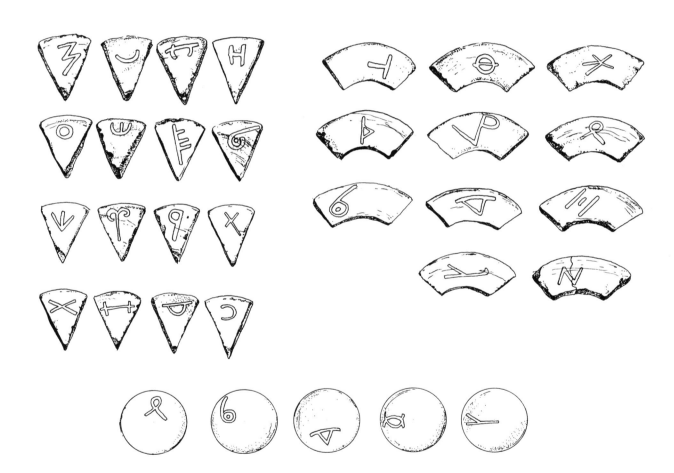

## Arminna West · Classic Christian Townsite · Room A–U–31
## Details of Column Bricks

Fig. 12. Details of column bricks from room 31, "The Public Building"

the lower rising to the west, the upper to the south (pl. IVd).

Room 37 measured *ca.* 9.15 x 2.75 m. It was connected to room 31 by a doorway 75 cm. in width in its north wall. A small series of rather poorly constructed screen walls were constructed at a later date in its southwest corner (pl. Va). Their purpose is not known. The floor of the room lay at *ca.* 126.50 m., some 10 cm. below the floor of room 31. A somewhat more carefully constructed wall, also of slightly later date than the Public Building generally, blocked the doorway (70 cm. in width) in the southwest corner of the room. Again, the purpose of this wall is not known.

Room 38, access to which was gained from the yard east of the Public Building by a 60 cm. wide doorway, measured 5.55 x 2.70 m. There were three niches, similar to those in rooms 31, 32, and 33, in the east and west walls of the room. Two others, extending to floor level, 1.10 m. wide, were constructed in the south and east walls. All were carefully plastered and whitewashed. The floor level was identical to that of room 31. There were no features.

Room 1, which effectively joined the Public Building and the 3–4–5 complex, measured 6.00 x *ca.* 2.50 m. (pl. Vd). We have already shown, from architectural evidence, that the room was built shortly after the room 3–4–5 unit, and, since room 1 was contemporaneous with the Public Building generally, we can extend this relative chronological sequence to include the entire southwest corner of area A–U.

The function of room 1 remains somewhat unclear. It is possible that it served as a sort of storage area for the Public Building. Certainly it did not form a functionally integral part of the general structure since its only entrance (60 cm. in width) opened directly into the yard east of room 33, rather than into the Building proper. It is, in a sense, a contemporaneous annex. Mr. Wojciech Kolataj, architect with the American Research Center in Egypt, has suggested that the structure at the east end of the room may indicate its use as a toilet similar to those to be found in contemporary Nubian houses. The architect's original report would tend to substantiate such an interpretation since the stairs in this corner did not extend above the present height of *ca.* 1.00 m., obviously insufficient to provide access to a roof or second story.

## II: Area "C–U"

Area C–U is a small portion of the Townsite which lies northeast of room A–U–13 (pl. VI, VII). It consisted of eight well-built and well-preserved rooms, all filled from floor to surface with wind-blown sand. The walls of the rooms were sufficiently well-preserved to show the springers of the barrel vaults, and all of the rooms were roofed in this fashion. Sherds were relatively scarce in the fill above the floors but were of a Classic Christian date.

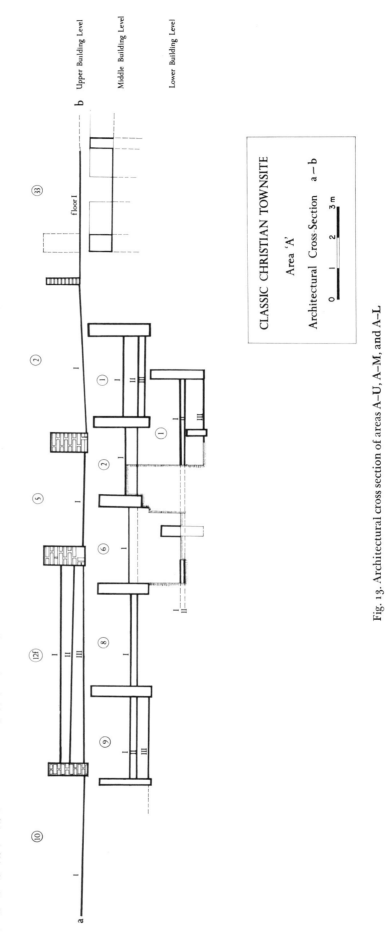

CLASSIC CHRISTIAN TOWNSITE

Area 'A'

Architectural Cross-Section a – b

Fig. 13. Architectural cross section of areas A–U, A–M, and A–L

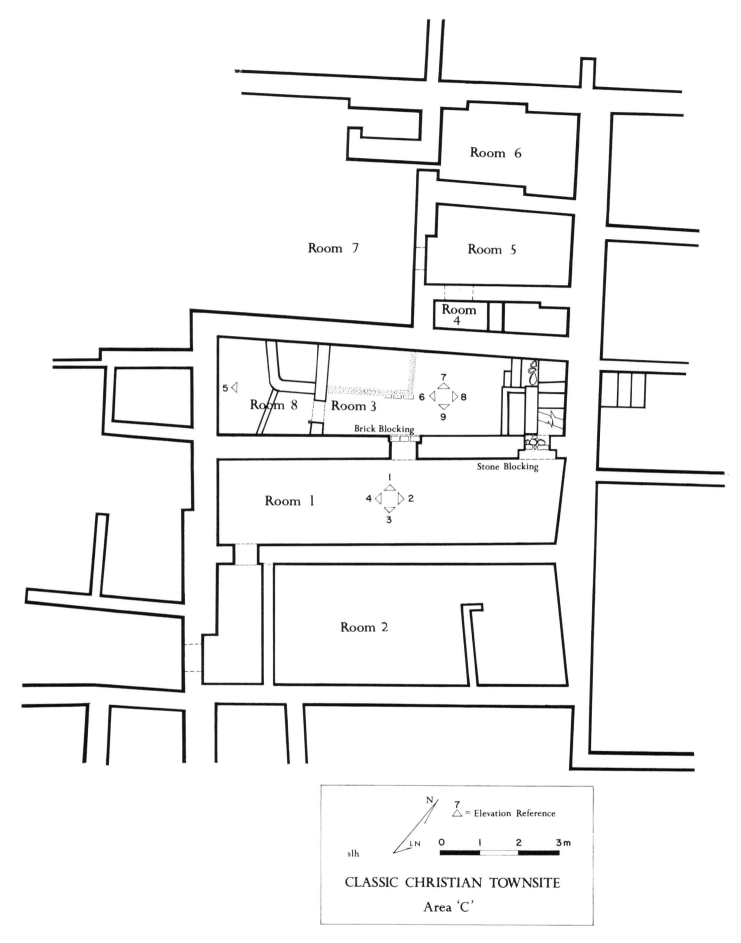

Room 6

Room 7    Room 5

Room 4

5 ◁    Room 8    Room 3    6 ◁    7 △ ▷ 8 ▽ 9
Brick Blocking

Stone Blocking

Room 1    1 △ 4 ◁ ▷ 2 ▽ 3

Room 2

N
7
△ = Elevation Reference

slh    L N    0    1    2    3 m

CLASSIC CHRISTIAN TOWNSITE
Area 'C'

Fig. 14. Plan of Upper Building Level, Area "C"

No systematic collection of sherds from this area was available for laboratory analysis and the area has therefore been excluded from the more detailed ceramic analysis presented in Part 3 of this report.

Excavation of area C–U was conducted during the 1962 field season. Since he was not present during this work, the author has based the following descriptions upon the field notes of other expedition members, particularly those of Mr. Nicholas Millet and Mr. Bruce Trigger.

### Individual Room Descriptions

*Room C–U–1 (pl. VIIc, XIc)*

Beneath a deep layer of wind-blown sand and fallen mud brick, the floor of room 1 lay at *ca.* 125.00 m. above sea level. The walls of the room were well-preserved to *ca.* 50 cm. above the springers and were covered with a layer of mud plaster, two to four centimeters thick. A small archway at the south end of the room, which led into room C–U–2, was blocked with mud bricks, and two others, at the north end (pl. VIIa), were similarly sealed off, the northernmost by the addition of a stairway in room C–U–3. A stone door socket was found in the fill near the center of the room at a depth of 126.00 m. Fragments of a terra-cotta basin, 75 cm. in diameter and 10 cm. deep, lay on the floor adjacent to the northernmost arched doorway. On the south wall of the room was a Late Christian cross, cut deep into the plaster.

*Room C–U–2 (pl. VIIb)*

The addition of a small east-west cross wall made two rooms of this structure. The northern portion yielded an incised jar (fig. 46i), which contained the remains of an infant burial. It lay in the northwest corner of the room and was in the floor. The floor level was almost identical to that of room C–U–1, and consisted of compact silt and mud.

The south wall of the room, like all other walls in this area, was covered with a heavy mud plaster. An archway at its east end led to a small chamber and a stairway rising to the west, up to what was either the roof or a second story. Immediately to the west of the door was the name of St. Michael, deeply incised in the mud plaster. An almost identical inscription was found on the mud covering the springers of the west wall (pl. VIIb). There were no features in the room.

*Rooms C–U–3 and C–U–8 (pl. VI)*

Rooms 3 and 8 were separated by a well-constructed wall with an archway at its eastern end which was constructed shortly after the major walls of the room (pl. VIa). The unit formed by rooms 3 and 8 measured 6.75 x 13.75 m. and entrance to it was gained by a staircase at the northern end of room 3. The five treads descended westward

from either the roof or an upper story, and two additional treads, which descended southward, led onto the floor of the room. This staircase was a later addition to the room, perhaps contemporaneous with the wall separating rooms 3 and 8. Prior to its construction, access was gained through two small archways from room 1, the southernmost of which has been blocked by mud brick, the northernmost by the staircase (pl. VIIa).

All of the walls in these rooms were covered by a two to four centimeter thick coat of mud plaster covered with a thin whitewash. Of particular interest was the treatment of the arch through the divider wall (pl. VIc). It was formed with an inlaid border of pebbles, and on either side and on the top were small crosses, again formed by pebbles stuck into the plaster.

A low step in the doorway led from room 3 to the higher floor level of room 8 (the floor of room 3 being *ca.* 125.00 m., that in room 8, *ca.* 125.30 m.). A small door socket lay *in situ* in the floor.

Room 8 was curiously quartered by low walls, one or two bricks in height (pl. VIb), which lay directly upon the floor. Their function is not known. A small wall running north-south was also found in room 3 and formed a large, low platform against the room's west wall. (A bowl from C–U–8 is shown in pl. Xb.)

*Rooms C–U–4, C–U–5, C–U–6, and C–U–7*

Room 4 formed a narrow (1.50 m. wide) foyer or hallway which connected the doorway of room C–U–5 with other rooms to the north. The floor was at *ca.* 125.00 m.; there were no features or objects in the room.

Both rooms C–U–5 and C–U–6 measured 2.25 x 3.50 m. Access to room 5 was gained by a 75 cm. wide doorway leading from room 4. A stone lintel formed the top of the door, and on its eastern surface were incised two crude signs, probably the Coptic *M*. There were no features.

A second archway led through room 5's south wall to room C–U–7, more aptly described as the northern extension of a large courtyard. In its northwest corner was a badly broken oven similar to those recorded in area A–U (see, e.g., pl. VIId).

### III: Area "N–U"

Excavation of a series of rooms adjacent to a major east-west wall of the Townsite, lying *ca.* 80 m. south of the Meroitic houses and Christian church reported by Trigger in volume 2 of this series and 55 m. north of area "A," has revealed a complex of pottery, stratigraphy, and architecture which appears, in many ways, to be representative of the Classic Christian period of the Townsite generally (pl. VIII).

In most cases, these rooms were filled with a layer of

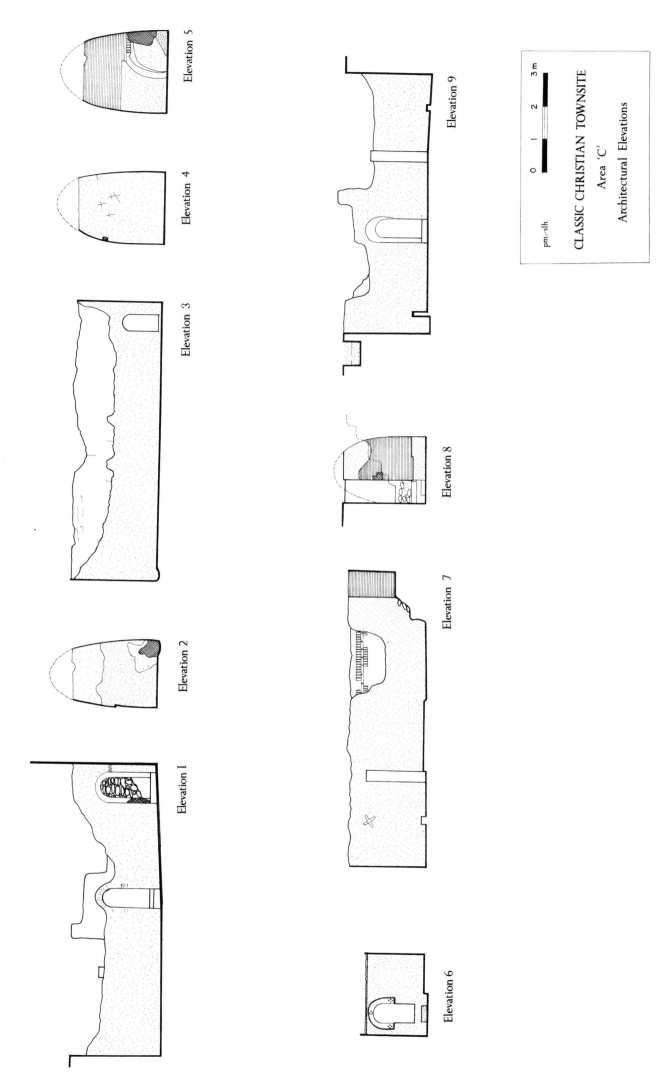

Elevation 5

Elevation 4

Elevation 3

Elevation 2

Elevation 1

Elevation 9

Elevation 8

Elevation 7

Elevation 6

CLASSIC CHRISTIAN TOWNSITE
Area 'C'
Architectural Elevations

0    1    2    3 m

Fig. 15. Architectural elevations, Area "C"

wind-blown sand and a thinner layer of dirt and silt. The area designated N–U–Forecourt, however, revealed a different stratigraphic picture which is described below.

Time did not permit excavation of area N–U below the floor level of the Upper Building, but it seems quite likely that here, as in area "A," earlier building complexes lay beneath these structures.

### Individual Room Descriptions

#### N–U–Forecourt (pl. VIIIb, f)

The forecourt area lay immediately west of the walls of room N–U–1 and north of one of the site's major east-west walls. There were apparently no walls on its north side nor any additional structures to its west. The forecourt probably served as a main entrance to the Upper Building complex and perhaps provided access from this unit to the Church and related structures to the north. A door through the main wall at the south of the forecourt, originally 2.75 m. in width, was twice blocked, once with mud brick which reduced its width to 1.25 m., and again with stone and mud which sealed it completely. The only floor in the forecourt lay at 123.55 m. and consisted of compact silt and mud.

A stratigraphic profile of the forecourt revealed three strata above this floor, and nine strata below it, consisting of alternating layers of wind-blown or heavily compacted sand and silt mixed with some ash. The pottery from these strata was thoroughly mixed and, since they were therefore impossible to date, we have not described them in detail. With the exception of stratum 1, of wind-blown sand, the deposits in the room would seem to represent a large refuse deposit of relatively late times.

#### Room N–U–1

Measuring 2.50 x 1.90 m., room 1 lay immediately east of the forecourt area. The room was covered by a low barrel vault, and the springers were clearly visible on the east wall.

The room had only one floor, at ca. 123.60 m., and the foundations of the north, west, and east walls lay slightly below this, at ca. 123.50 m. The southern wall extended down to ca. 123.25 m. Two strata lay above the floor, a deep layer of wind-blown sand and, below this, a level of dark brown silts.

#### Room N–U–2 (pl. VIIId)

Situated between rooms N–U–1 and N–U–3, room 2 was separated from N–U–5 by a thick screen wall, the foundations of which lay 50 cm. above the foundations of the east and west walls. The springers of the east and west walls were still visible at ca. 124.40 m.

Stratigraphically, N–U–2 was similar to N–U–Forecourt. Below a thick layer of sand there was a stratum of dark brown silt and earth which extended to the floor at ca. 123.50 m. The floor was of compacted silt and mud.

#### Room N–U–3

At its northern end, room 3 opened into room 5. The wall between it and room 4 at one time completely separated the two rooms, but the removal of bricks from its north end has formed a doorway ca. 1.30 m. in width. The room measured 2.25 m. in width and 5.50 m. in length and was vaulted. The springers on the west wall lay at the same level as those in room 2. The stratigraphy of the room was identical to other rooms in area "N," and the floor lay at ca. 123.50 m.

In the southeast corner of the room was a small platform ca. 7 cm. high which measured 170 x 100 cm., formed of compact mud and lined with a series of well-worn mud bricks. The platform (pl. VIIIe) was similar to those found in various rooms of area A–U and, like those features, perhaps served the same purpose as the low cooking platforms found in contemporary Nubian houses (pl. XIIId, Xc).

#### Room N–U–4

The stratigraphy of N–U–4 was slightly different from that of other rooms in this area, for beneath the usual thick level of wind-blown sand (here almost one meter deep) there was a 30 cm. stratum of dark brown earth which contained small quantities of ash, and beneath this, a 20 to 30 cm. deep stratum of well-compacted light brown earth. The floor, of compacted silt and mud, lay beneath level 3 at 123.55 m. Within this third stratum, in the southwest corner of the room, was a heavy concentration of blue-gray ash, 15 cm. thick and about 1.25 m. wide. The ash deposit at one time entirely covered a small mud brick platform in this corner (25 cm. high and ca. 75 x 125 cm.), but was at some time removed so that only a thin layer of it remained adhering to the west wall of the room. The source of this ash is not known, although it resembles that associated with various ovens in the site. Most likely, the room was abandoned for a short time, the ash dumped here and then later removed when the room was re-occupied. The platform (pl. VIIIg) which lay under the ash was perhaps used for cooking, in the same way as those in contemporary Nubian houses (pl. XIIId) and that in room N–U–3.

The east and west walls of the room appeared contemporaneous and at one time abutted the east-west wall to their north. Both have had bricks removed from their northern end, however, to provide a passage between rooms N–U–8 and N–U–3. There was another doorway at the south end of the east wall which provided access to the room from the stairwell to the east (pl. VIIIh). The door was blocked by broken brick and stone, and this was perhaps the reason for the later removal of

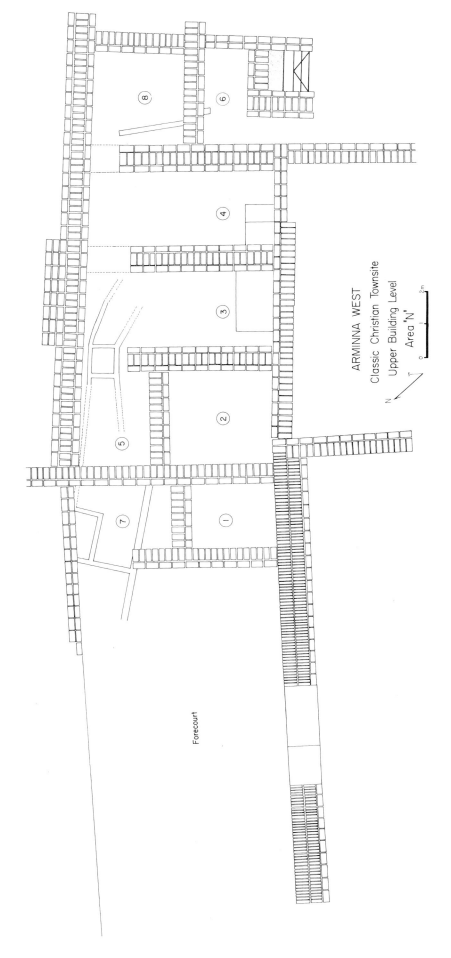

ARMINNA WEST
Classic Christian Townsite
Upper Building Level
Area "N"

Fig. 16. Plan of Upper Building Level, Area "N"

brick at the wall's north end. The room measured 5.25 x 2.25 m. and was vaulted. Fragments of a Coptic stela (number 376, pl. Xf) were found in the room's fill, level 1.

## Room N–U–5 (pl. VIIIc)

N–U–5 was a small room lying immediately north of N–U–2. Stratigraphically, it was similar to N–U–1 and N–U–2, although sherds were extremely scarce in both strata. On the floor, which was at *ca.* 123.55 m., a small arc formed by four mud bricks lay in the southeast corner. The passage between N–U–5 and N–U–3 was slightly lower than the floor level of either room (*ca.* 123.45 m.) and was paved with three large slabs of sandstone which extended well into room N–U–3. In this same area, adjacent to and slightly below the sandstone slabs, there were indications of a series of small walls similar in form to those in the floor of room N–U–7. It would appear that these were all part of the same structural series as were those in N–U–8, and all predated the major walls of area "N."

## Room N–U–6

Time did not permit complete excavation of this room although the remnants of a staircase at its western end were cleared. The stairway led to either a higher room or perhaps to a second story. Only four treads were still intact. These descended to the north, apparently at one time giving access to the doorway into room N–U–6 and to a passageway leading northward. The stairway appeared contemporaneous with the wall between N–U–4 and N–U–6, and was at some later date blocked by the addition of a small wall which appeared contemporaneous with the south and west walls of room N–U–8. The stratigraphy in the room followed the pattern of levels 1 and 2 in N–U–Forecourt.

## Room N–U–7 (pl. XIf)

Beneath two strata identical to those of rooms N–U–1 and N–U–Forecourt, floor I lay at *ca.* 123.45 m. On the floor there were several small structures apparently built some time prior to construction of the room's major walls. In the northwest corner a small structure one mud brick in height suggested the base of some type of storage bin. Its foundation lay at 123.40 m., some two to three centimeters below the thin floor of the room. The row of mud bricks which formed the west wall of the bin continued southward where they joined a similarly constructed east-west wall which ran under the main east wall of the room. This wall unfortunately broke off to the west, and its relation to the west wall of N–U–7 could not be ascertained. That these small, rather crudely built structures precede the construction of the east, west, and north walls of N–U–7 is certain. But their chronological relationship

to the south wall of the room, and consequently to the walls of area "N" generally, is not known.

## Room N–U–8

N–U–8 was the easternmost of the rooms excavated in this area. It lay east of N–U–4 and north of N–U–6, and its stratigraphy was typical of the area, i.e., two strata identical to levels 1 and 2 of N–U–Forecourt.

The floor of the room lay at *ca.* 123.60 m. On it, in the southwest corner of the room, was a small platform of mud, *ca.* 5 cm. high, on which were placed two mud bricks. Within the small enclosure thus formed was a small oil jar, number N–U–8(1).

Slightly to the west of the platform was a badly broken, crudely built wall of which only the lowest two courses of bricks remained. The wall ran north to south and, since it lay within the floor of the room, was presumably contemporaneous with similar structures in N–U–7 (pl. Xd).

### IV: Discussion

Despite the slightly higher foundations of the walls of rooms A–U 3, 4, and 5, it seems fairly certain that they are the earliest of the rooms constructed in area A–U and probably among the earliest constructed in the Upper Building generally. The sherds from these rooms are almost exclusively of Early Christian date, with a few specimens of the Transitional Period included, while those from adjacent structures are of Classic and Late Christian times. Architecturally, the construction of adjacent walls in rooms A–U 6, 12f, and 12g suggests an early date for the 3–4–5 complex, while the architectural relationship between room 3 and room 1 definitely indicates that room 1 and the Public Building as a whole were built after that unit. Thus, the pottery within the rooms and the structural relationships of the building with surrounding structures indicate its chronological priority in area A–U, and more specifically, as we shall now attempt to demonstrate, give it an Early Christian date.

Adams[6] notes that house construction during his Transitional and Early Christian I periods was quite crude and that "herringbone" architecture was common. However, during his Early Christian II period, which he tentatively dates from A.D. 750 to 850, he notes that although the major part of the architecture remains unchanged, "more substantial construction of mud brick, with vaulted ceilings, for larger buildings"[7] does also occur. Such structures have been noted by Shinnie at Debeira West[8] and by Adams at Faras,[9] and there is some degree of similarity between them and our room 3–4–5

---

6. Adams, *Kush* XII (1964): 241–47; see esp. 243–44.
7. *Ibid.*, p. 244.
8. Shinnie, *Kush* XII (1964): 208–15.
9. Adams, *Kush* IX (1961): 30–43.

unit. Both in terms of pottery and of architecture, therefore, it seems most probable that this unit was constructed during Adams' Early Christian II period.

Although the ceilings of this unit were originally vaulted, there was no mud brick debris found in the rooms. For later occupations—and we know that the rooms were re-used at least once—there is no evidence that the building was covered by any permanent sort of structure. In examining the evidence, both Dr. Bruce Trigger and I have wondered if perhaps later inhabitants did not make use of roofing material similar to the easily portable and re-usable reed mats and small pole rafters still in use in the area today. A photograph of this type of roofing materials in use at Abu Simbel village in 1964 is shown in pl. XIIIb.[10]

The purpose served by these rooms, which at the time of their occupation formed a single, isolated unit (perhaps of two stories), cannot be stated with certainty because of the lack of associated artifacts and features. Nevertheless, the rooms bear some resemblance to houses recently excavated at Debeira West in the Sudan[11] and to houses of a somewhat later date at Kasr-Ico.[12]

The dating of the Public Building is on somewhat less solid ground since artifacts and features are extremely rare. From architectural details and from the pottery found directly above and within the floors of the rooms, however, there seems good reason to assume that only a brief period of time elapsed between construction of rooms 3–4–5 (and of room 7 which is contemporaneous with them) and the construction of the Public Building. If this is correct, then the Public Building may also be assigned an Early Christian II date.

We have already stated that the term "Public Building" was chosen because of the desire to avoid any more committal term. But in addition to these rather negative reasons for its selection, there are several positive ones as well. We have already noted that the interpretation of the complex as a house, castle, palace, or church raises more questions than it answers. The non-private nature of the structure, however, could well account for such factors as the number of doors opening directly into the courtyard, the rather surprising regularity and formalism of the plan, the open courtyard with the column or pedestal in its center, the niches in many of the walls (which could have served as seats), and the relative isolation of room 1. To what purpose such a public structure might have been put is not known, however, and this lack of knowledge is the major reason the interpretation is couched in such vague terms.

It is interesting to note that the southern portion of the Plain of Arminna contains very little of Early Christian date while the northern portion is largely of this period.[13] During Classic and Late Christian times, almost exactly the reverse is true. There is no indication that the site as a whole was ever completely abandoned, even for a brief period of time. Rather, there is every indication of continuity and continuous occupation even, perhaps, from Late Meroitic times. The population movements one can discover occur within the site, when families moved from one house to another, from one area of the site to another, as buildings became non-functional, or as economic, social, or ecological factors dictated.

During early and middle Classic Christian times, areas "C" and "N" seem to have been flourishing (although the length of their occupation is not known) and from architectural and ceramic evidence, this would seem to have been the period of greatest activity for the Townsite as a whole. The structures in area "C" seem clearly to be those of a large, well-constructed house, and other, similar structures can be seen on the surface of the entire Townsite area. Houses of this type are extremely common in Nubia, the closest similar examples of approximately the same date being at Gebel Adda.[14] The pottery from this area and from area "N" was a rather amorphous mixture, and although it points in both cases to a Classic Christian date there is no way in which the two can be more exactly equated. It would seem from the architectural evidence at hand, however, that area "N" is somewhat later than "C," although perhaps by only a brief period. What function the area "N" rooms served is still uncertain. Most likely, they formed a foundation story (and storage area?) for some building above them.

We have already seen that the Public Building and the room 3–4–5 complex were the earliest structures in area A–U. Following them, rooms 6 and 9 appear next in order, room 6 perhaps having served as a workroom or oven for the later periods of use of rooms 3–4–5, room 9 at that time serving as a courtyard. Sherds from these two rooms are generally of Early Christian or Classic Christian date.

During Classic Christian times, perhaps only slightly earlier than the occupation of the house in area C–U, the complex of rooms A–U–12a–g was constructed. These structures are considerably less well-built than the other rooms of the site, but would not seem to reflect any major change in economic or architectural considerations during the period. Perhaps intended as a dwelling, perhaps as workrooms, they seem in any case to have been constructed as only semi-permanent structures.

Following construction of the room 12 complex and

10. See also Trigger 1967: part 8.

11. Shinnie, *Kush* XII (1964): 208–15.

12. Presedo Velo, 1963; see fig. 7, especially plans of houses A and B. A general plan of Abkanarti Island is to be found in Almagro, *et al., Kush* XI (1963): 175–79, fig. 9.

13. Trigger, 1967.

14. N. B. Millet (1966: personal communication). Of particular interest is his House 337.

the house in area "C" came rooms A–U 8, 10, and 11, which represent dwelling-units of the late Classic Christian or Late Christian periods. They seem, despite their late date, to precede slightly the construction of room 13.

The area to the west of area "A," including the covered passageway (pl. IIId), is most likely contemporaneous with the house of area "C," i.e., of Classic Christian times, a date which may be confirmed by the presence of a sandstone column capital found *ca.* 50 cm. below the surface immediately northwest of the passageway's western limits. Where this capital originally came from is not known, but it may indicate the presence of a church of Classic Christian date within the Townsite complex (pl. IIIf).

It should be noted here that the pipe section shown in pl. XIb was found *in situ* placed vertically within the vaulted ceiling of a room southwest of the passageway's western limits, *ca.* 25 cm. below the surface. Its position would indicate its use either as a smoke-hole (i.e., a chimney) or as an opening for a room in which something like grain may have been stored. (This pipe section is not included in the ceramic typology in Part 3.)

# Chapter Two:
# Middle and Lower Building Levels

BENEATH THE FOUNDATIONS of the Upper Building level in area "A" two additional levels of major importance were uncovered (pl. IX). Directly beneath A–U lay what we have termed the Middle Building level, a series of rooms and courtyards of Late Meroitic times which were later re-used during the X-Group period. There is every reason to believe that the Middle Building was nearly as extensive as area A–U, for in addition to the eleven rooms we uncovered below rooms A–U–3, A–U–4, A–U–5, A–U–9, and A–U–12g, sections of additional walls were uncovered below other parts of room A–U–12, below room A–U–11, room A–U–31 (pl. Vc), and below traces of Upper Building walls at the eastern edge of the site.

### Individual Room Descriptions
### Room A–M–1 (figs. 13 and 18)

Measuring 4.80 x 2.60 m., room A–M–1 was one of the largest and best constructed rooms of the Middle Building level. The walls of the room were an average of 40 cm. in thickness and were covered with three coats of fine quality plaster.

Lying below the compact sands of room A–U–2 level 4, and of A–M–1 level 1, floor I consisted of well-compacted silts with a thin covering of mud. The floor lay at 125.35 m. and the outer layer of the three plaster coats applied to the walls curved onto this floor and was contemporaneous with it. There were no features associated with the floor, which seems to represent a re-use of the room after the vaulted ceiling had collapsed.

Beneath floor I, level 2 consisted of sand and large numbers of broken mud bricks and plaster fragments from the vaulted ceiling. The bricks from this vault measured 36 x 18 x 8 cm. and were slightly tapered.

Floor II, at 124.85 m., was contemporaneous with the middle of the three layers of plaster and was in use prior to the roof's collapse. There were no features. It was at this time that the doorway between rooms A–M–1 and A–M–4 was made narrower (from 1.20 to 0.60 m.) by the addition of a mud brick blocking within the doorway.

Beneath level 3, which consisted of fine sand and silt, floor III was a thick layer of silt covered with a thin mud plaster. It lay at 124.60 m., *ca.* ten centimeters above the

foundation of the walls, and was contemporaneous with the initial coat of plaster applied to the walls, a very thin layer of whitewash applied to a thick coat of mud. Floor III represents the initial occupation of the room, and the doorways into rooms A–M–2 and A–M–4 opened onto this level. There was no sill in either doorway. It might be noted that the wall between A–M–1 and A–M–2—A–M–3 is slightly later than the other walls of this room (see below).

### Rooms A–M–2 and A–M–3
### (fig. 18; see also fig. 13, pl. IXa, b)

These rooms, of almost identical size (A–M–2 is 1.40 x 2.40 m., A–M–3 is 1.60 x 2.40 m.), lay adjacent to, and were accessible from, room A–M–1. The wall separating them from A–M–1 appears to have been built after the initial use of floor III of that room but before its abandon-

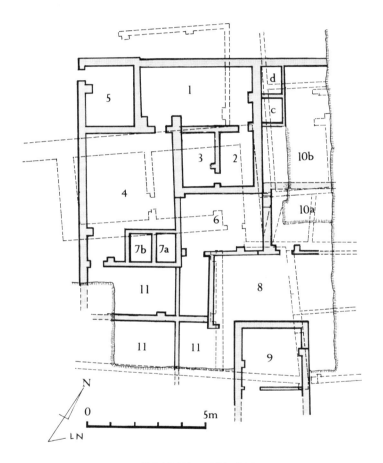

ARMINNA WEST
Classic Christian Townsite
Area "A"

MIDDLE BUILDING
LEVEL

( Dotted Lines= Walls of A-U-Buildings )

Fig. 17. Plan of the Middle Building Level

ment and before the deposition of level 3 and floor II. This wall, and the smaller wall separating rooms A–M–2 and A–M–3, had foundations at 124.55 m., while those of room A–M–1 (north, south, and west walls) lay at 124.50 m.

Floor I of both rooms lay at 125.18 m. and the rooms were joined by a 50 cm. wide doorway, the mud brick sill of which lay at 125.31 m.

Against the south wall of A–M–2 was a 20 cm. high mud brick platform, used perhaps for storage or as a workbench. In the northwest corner of room A–M–3 a small pit had been dug in the floor and in it had been placed a large storage jar (pl. IXb).

Of architectural interest was the point at which the wall between rooms 2 and 3 joined the wall of A–M–1. Here, an additional section of wall, roughly semicircular in form, was built to provide structural support for the union of the walls, but perhaps also to serve as a storage bin. Numerous X-Group goblets (form class "D") were removed from its fill (see pl. Xa).

As noted above, the construction of the walls between A–M–2—A–M–3 and A–M–1 was slightly later than floor III of room A–M–1. Floor II of rooms 2 and 3, a very thin layer of compacted silts, lay at approximately the same level as A–M–1 floor III and was probably contemporaneous with it. Floor I of rooms 2 and 3 appears to have been contemporaneous with A–M–1 floor I.

Sherds from the two rooms were almost exclusively of X-Group date although a few Early Christian sherds were found in the upper part of level 1.

### Room A–M–4

The room measured 4.20 x 3.80 m. and had a 1.80 x 1.00 m. entrance hall at its east end, adjacent to rooms A–M–7a–b. The floor of the room lay at 124.60 m. and, with the exception of a low (25 cm.) bench about 1.50 m. long against the room's north wall, there were no features. It should be noted that the eastern half of the north wall, and the eastern wall of the entrance hall were all somewhat later additions to the site and followed the construction of rooms A–M–1, 2, 3, and 5. Sherds were of X-Group date.

### Room A–M–5 (fig. 18)

Above the level of floor I, which lay at *ca.* 125.15 m., was a layer of sand and large quantities of fallen mud brick, presumably from the collapsed vaulted roof of the room. The bricks were of similar size and shape to those found between floors I and II of room A–M–1, and it seems reasonable to assume that floor II of A–M–1 and floor I of A–M–5 were contemporaneous, although there was about 30 cm. difference in the elevations.

The room was excavated to the level of floor I. Sherds

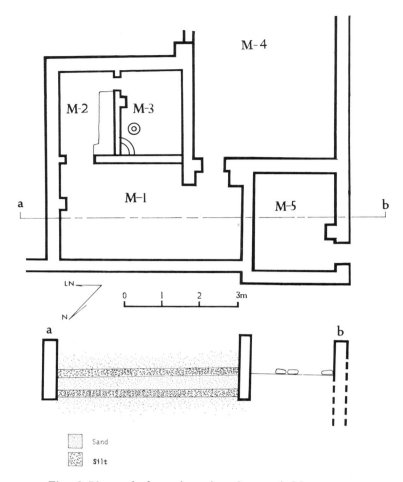

Fig. 18. Plan and schematic section of rooms A–M–1, 2, 3, 5

from level I and this floor were of X-Group date. There were no features.

### Room A–M–6

The floor of this room, lying at 125.07 m., was sufficiently lower than the floor of A–M–11 (125.30 m.) to have required the construction of two low steps at the entrance. These steps, at 125.25 m. and at 125.14 m., were of mud brick and both they and the door sill (125.28 m.) were covered with a heavy layer of mud plaster. There were no features on the floor, but in the northeast corner of the room a layer of mud bricks (36 x 24 x 7 cm.) measuring 1.75 x 1.50 m. was found 50 cm. below the floor (which lay at 124.56 m.).

Immediately beneath this mud brick structure was a storage bin, formed by placing two pottery pipes 50 cm. in diameter and 54 m. long one atop the other. The bin extended from 124.45 m. to a depth of 123.39 m., well into the rooms of the Lower Building level. From within the pit ten broken and whole goblets (form class "D") and other pottery vessels were removed (see pl. Xa and IXf). Adjacent to the storage pit were the tops of the irregular wall series of room A–L–2. These will be discussed later in this chapter.

31

It should be noted that the brick structure above this storage pit lay above the level of the foundations of either the room's east wall (the foundation of which lay at 124.42 m.) or the west wall (at 124.73 m.). Why this bin would have been placed so far beneath the floor level is unclear and its purpose remains unknown. Certainly, however, it was associated with the floor level, although it was constructed some time after the floor had been laid down. Sherds were of X-Group date.

### Storage Bins A–M–7, a and b

A–M–7a and A–M–7b lay adjacent to the entrance hall of room A–M–4 and were part of the structures in room 4's corner which were built some time after the main walls of the room were constructed.

Both bins were filled with sand and broken mud brick and the floor of both lay at 125.07 m., only slightly below the average floor level of A–M–4. In A–M–7b a very thin layer of mud covered the room at *ca.* 125.55 m. and on this thin layer was a fired clay offering table (pl. XIIa). From slightly below the mud layer a pottery lamp was recovered (number 541) and is shown in fig. 47c.

Sherds from these storage bins, though scarce, were of X-Group date.

### Room A–M–8

The first floor of A–M–8 appears to represent a late re-use of the room. It lay at 125.50 m. and on it, in the southwest corner, were the badly broken remains of a small and rather poorly made oven, similar in form to those of the Upper Building level (rooms A–U–6, A–U–11, etc.). The oven was surrounded by a single row of mud bricks measuring 34 x 10 x 8 cm. Beneath floor I, the room was filled with a heavy layer of sand and ash, extending down to floor II at 124.95 m. A small wall at this level separated rooms A–M–8 and A–M–10. Also on floor II, against the room's west wall, a small 5 cm. high platform was found, perhaps a support or storage bench of some kind.

Beneath floor II, a deposit of almost pure ash extended down to the foundations of the walls at 124.35 m. The ash seems to represent oven refuse, but from which oven it comes is not known. Sherds were again of X-Group date.

### Room A–M–9 (fig. 19; pl. IXc, d, e).

The first floor level of the room lay at 125.05 m. A doorway in the room's north wall had been blocked by mud and mud brick, apparently some time after the laying down of floor I. In the southwest corner of the room was a well-constructed oven (fig. 19 and pl. IXc, d, e) in a remarkably fine state of preservation. The oven had been built with a carefully fashioned ceramic interior covered with small mud brick and a heavy coat of well-made mud plaster.

A heavy layer of almost pure ash separated floor I from floor II at 124.81 m. There were no features on this floor, but the foundations of the oven described above extended to this depth and the oven was presumably contemporaneous with the floor level.

Floor III, at 124.40 m., lay beneath a layer of ash and sand. The only feature was a small but well-built platform of mud brick and mud in the extreme northeast corner of the room, the top of which lay at the same level as floor II but the foundations of which indicated its association with floor III. On this platform were found over thirty small round pebbles, 3 to 5 cm. in diameter, perhaps used as burnishing stones.

Below floor III, level 4 was of sand and silt and the tops of the walls from the Lower Building level were found only about 10 cm. below the floor.

Room A–M–9, as we have noted, was a remarkably well-built room. The walls were carefully and evenly covered with a 2 cm. thick layer of mud plaster; the oven was a fine example of careful construction; the floors were of smooth, thick layers of mud; the platform in the corner was covered with mud bricks, carefully laid with joints filled with mortar to provide a very smooth working surface.

Lying on top of the oven was a circular piece of fired clay, *ca.* 30 cm. in diameter and 4 cm. thick, resembling what some have called pottery palettes, but what might more accurately be termed cooking surfaces or griddles.

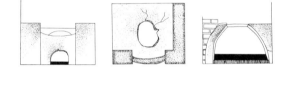

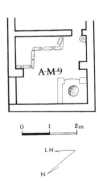

Fig. 19. Plan of room A–M–9 and details of oven

### Room A–M–10 (a, b, c, and d)

This area, the northern limit of excavation at this level, consisted of two rooms and two small storage bins similar in form to A–M–7a and 7b. Rooms A–M–10a and 10b were not excavated below the level of the floors except to check foundation levels at several corners. Storage bins

A–M–10c and 10d were filled with sterile sand to a depth of *ca.* 124.70 m., at which level a poorly made mud floor was found. There were no artifacts.

*Room A–M–11*

Originally, A–M–11 appears to have been two rather large rooms which were later divided by the construction of a crude east-west cross wall. Their floor levels lay at *ca.* 125.00 m. There were no features and no artifacts.

In general, the construction of the Middle Building level was of good quality. The walls were carefully laid, well-plastered, and well laid out; the floors were generally of thick mud, solid and level. The Late Meroitic date for this structure is in large part based upon the quality of the construction, but is confirmed by the presence of occasional Meroitic sherds in the otherwise X-Group strata and by the large quantities of Meroitic material in the level below the lower floors (which blends into level 1 of the Lower Building level).

The sequence of construction in the level is difficult to determine because of the small area encompassed by the excavation. Nevertheless, it would appear that rooms 1, 2, 3, and 5 were the first to be built in the area, and

perhaps served as a house for which rooms 4 and 6 then formed the courtyard. Following this, probably only shortly after, rooms 4, 6, 7, 9, and 10 were built, with the walls forming rooms 8 and 11 being still later additions.

*Rooms A–L–1 and A–L–2* (figs. 20, 21; pl. IXg)

During the last few days of the 1963 field season two small sections of area A–L were excavated and, although not sufficient to allow study of the architectural details of the buildings at this level, the excavation did provide materials for an understanding of the earlier periods of the site.

It seems likely that level "L" represents the earliest buildings in the Classic Christian Townsite, but excavation could not be extended into soil definitely known to be sterile because of the Nile water table which we reached at 122.20 m. and which made any further excavation impossible.

Room A–L–1 lay directly below A–M–1 and its first floor was reached at 123.50 m. There were no features on the floor. Beneath a layer of sand and silt lay floor II at 123.25 m., and again there were no features.

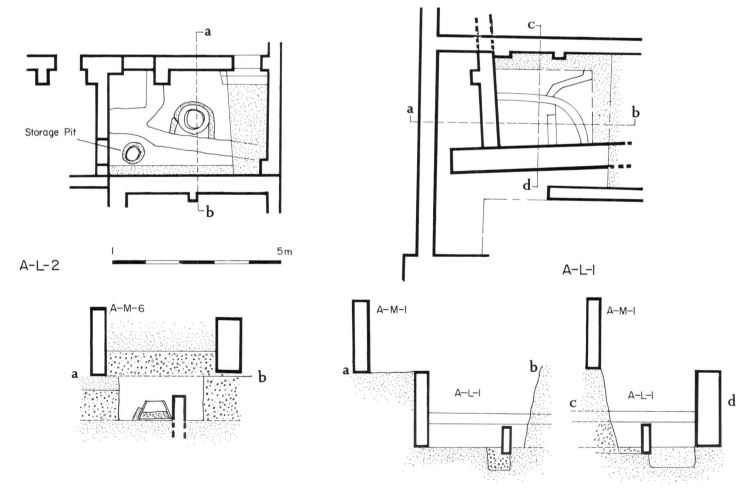

Fig. 20. Plans and sections, rooms A–L–1, 2

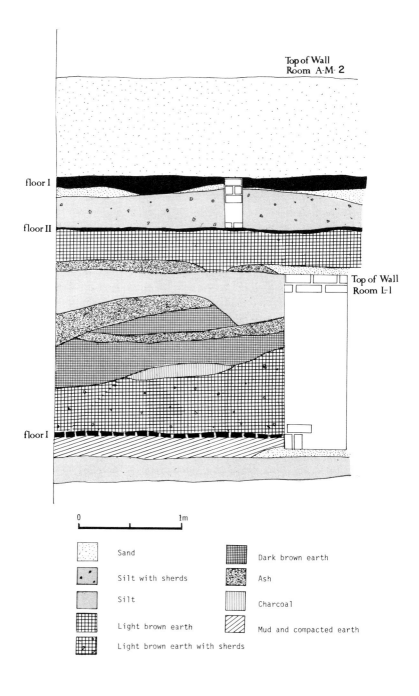

floor I

floor II

floor I

Top of Wall
Room A·M· 2

Top of Wall
Room L·1

0                    1m

| | Sand | | Dark brown earth |
| | Silt with sherds | | Ash |
| | Silt | | Charcoal |
| | Light brown earth | | Mud and compacted earth |
| | Light brown earth with sherds | | |

PROFILE OF WEST BAULK, ROOM A–L–1

Fig. 21. Stratigraphic profile of west baulk, room A–L–1

The main walls of the room had their foundations on floor III, at 122.75 m., while a strangely built series of secondary walls, the tops of which appeared at 123.15 m., extended slightly below floor III, to 122.60 m. All of these walls rested on foundations of mud and silt, while the level below floor III was of sand. Floor III itself was a well-built surface of mud brick, laid in a regular pattern over the entire room. It was extremely difficult, however, to outline the bricks since water had seeped into the level and materials were in a very poor state of preservation.

Room A–L–2 lay directly beneath A–M–6. In excavating the rooms of the Middle Building level, we found a deep storage pit in A–M–6 which extended below the foundations of the surrounding walls, to a depth of 123.39 m. The tops of the walls of A–L–2 extended well above this level, averaging 124.06 m. Time did not permit excavation to the foundations of these walls, but at *ca.* 124.00 m. the top of an oven similar in design to those of the Middle and Upper Building levels was found. Its foundation was at 123.44 m. The oven was built against a small wall running northeast and a number of Meroitic sherds were associated with the floor immediately around the oven. No other features were found.

Both architecturally and in terms of pottery, the remains of level A–L relate to structures excavated by Trigger at the northern end of the Plain of Arminna,[1] and there seems little need to do more here than to refer to Trigger's study of this period.

1. Trigger, 1967.

34

PART *3*

# THE POTTERY

*Chapter One:*

## Introduction

OF ALL THE CULTURAL products with which the Nubian archaeologist deals, few are quite as important as pottery. Occurring in abundance in almost every site from Neolithic times onward, it can be used as an indicator of cultural continuity or change, of isolation or contact, of contemporaneity or temporal variation. Pottery provides an almost unlimited medium of expression for various cultural, aesthetic preferences and, as a consequence, it is subject to continuous chronological and geographic variation. Adams has pointed out, for example, that "it has been the identification and plotting of minor stylistic changes more than any other factor that has permitted the highly refined ceramic dating now possible in some parts of the world."[1]

During recent years several Nubian sites have been excavated which have yielded great quantities of ceramic material, much of it in clearly stratified contexts. From this material, particularly that from the Faras Potteries (Sudanese Nubian site 24–E–21), William Adams has developed a detailed classification of X-Group and Christian ceramic forms, fabrics, styles, and wares, and excavation and analysis of other sites in Sudanese Nubia have tended to confirm his classificatory system and its chronological framework.[2] To date, however, there has been no opportunity to apply his system to materials from sites north of the Sudanese border, an application which is needed if the geographic variations in pottery form and date are to be made clear. To examine these variations in the ceramic sequence at Arminna West, to better define certain of the wares and fabrics described by Adams, and to study the Arminna West pottery simply within its own archaeological context, two methodological approaches have been used.

*Method of ceramic analysis.* The objectives given above both required that a statistically valid, representative sample of the ceramic material be taken from the Townsite, first to reflect the total sherd population, second, to provide a sufficient number of specimens to allow generalization and comparison with the form, style, fabric, and ware classifications of Adams. These samples were acquired by means of a continuous series of sortings and analyses in the field and laboratory. At the end of each day all the sherds from each room level were described, and those which appeared to be of particular diagnostic value (e.g., rim, base, or decorated sherds) were labelled and saved. At irregular intervals, as a large number of specimens was accumulated, another sorting by form, fabric, and decoration was conducted and a large sample of each recorded and saved. Finally, at the end of the season, a third selection was made which reduced the total of 35,000 excavated sherds to a sample of 5,000. This sample was shipped to the laboratory for more detailed ceramic analysis.

Since, during the final laboratory analysis, we were able to trace frequencies back through the earlier series of selections and descriptions, we can state with some confidence that the percentage figures given below, although based primarily upon our sample of 5,000 sherds, are also fairly accurate descriptions of the 35,000 sherds which comprised the original population.

For each of the sherds analyzed in the laboratory a record of the findspot was made and the specimen given a catalogue number. On a series of attribute forms a description of each sherd was prepared. The quality of firing was noted as good, fair, or poor. Texture was described as fine, medium, coarse, and the temper was identified. Hardness was tested by means of a Mohs' scale of hardness, and each sherd was placed in one of three categories: soft (hardness of 1 to 3.5); medium (hardness of 3.5 to 6.5); or hard (6.5 to 10.0). Color of both paste and slip was determined using the "Rock-Color Chart" of the Geological Society of America. This is an abbreviated version of the Munsell Color System long in use by archaeologists and is normally sufficiently complete for ceramic description. A full description of this chart is readily available, and Shepard[3] has given a thorough discussion of its use in her text. It may be of value, however, briefly to describe the function of these color charts, since it is from their use that our additions to many of Adams' ware descriptions have been effected.

The Munsell Color System, and all charts which follow its principles, make use of three variables of color: *hue,* the color's position in the spectrum; *value,* the lightness or darkness of the color; and *chroma,* the brightness or purity of the color. A series of symbols permits the description of these three variables for any color. Hue is

1. Adams, *Kush* X (1962): 245–88. See also Shepard, 1956. The basis for ceramic typologies such as that offered for Christian Nubia has been criticized by H. P. Newell and A. D. Krieger, 1949. Their objection to sherd-based rather than vessel-based typologies merits examination by anyone working with ceramic materials.

2. See, e.g., Shinnie, *Kush* XI (1963) and XII (1964).

3. Shepard, 1956.

designated by the first letter of the hue name and by a number indicating its position in the "hue range." Values are arranged numerically from 0 (black) to 10 (white).

TABLE 1. Selected Rock-Color Chart Notations and Descriptive Terms

| Hue | Notation | Common Name |
|---|---|---|
| 5R | 2/2 | Blackish red |
| | 2/6 | Very dark red |
| | 3/4 | Dusky red |
| | 4/2 | Grayish red |
| | 5/4 | Moderate red |
| | 6/2 | Pale pink |
| | 6/6 | Light red |
| | 7/4 | Moderate pink |
| | 8/2 | Grayish pink |
| 10R | 2/2 | Very dusky red |
| | 3/4 | Dark reddish brown |
| | 4/2 | Grayish red |
| | 5/4 | Pale reddish brown |
| | 6/2 | Pale red |
| | 7/4 | Moderate orange pink |
| | 8/2 | Grayish orange pink |
| 5YR | 2/2 | Dusky brown |
| | 3/4 | Moderate brown |
| | 5/2 | Pale brown |
| | 5/6 | Light brown |
| 10YR | 4/2 | Dark yellowish brown |
| | 5/4 | Moderate yellowish brown |
| | 6/6 | Dark yellowish orange |
| | 7/4 | Grayish orange |
| | 8/2 | Very pale orange |
| 5Y | 2/1 | Olive black |
| | 4/1 | Olive gray |
| | 8/1 | Yellowish gray |

Chroma is expressed numerically from 1 to 8, and value and chroma are given as a fraction. For example, the color 5R 5/8 is a red of medium hue, of medium value and high purity; 7R 8/5 is more orange, lighter, and grayer.[4] Although in some ways awkward, colors expressed in this standardized system are considerably easier to use for comparative studies than such terms as Dragon's Blood Red or Pacific Salmon Pink. However, to facilitate reference to Munsell Color designations, the U.S. National Bureau of Standards has assigned a series of descriptive terms to each hue-value-chroma combination. Those colors most frequently used in describing the pottery of Arminna West are listed together with their Rock-Color Chart, National Bureau of Standards names in Table 1.

In addition to these descriptions of the physical attributes of a vessel or sherd, each specimen was further described using the classificatory system of Adams.[5] If a vessel was found which could not comfortably be placed within his categories it was described in terms of the typologies utilized by P. L. Shinnie,[6] by Emery and Kirwan,[7] or by itself as an aberrant or separate form. Styles were designed in this same fashion. Ware descriptions represent both a utilization of Adams' system and our own physical analysis of the pottery. Few difficulties were encountered in this latter phase of work since Adams' fabric categories are remarkably complete and his synthesis of form, fabric, and style into wares generally inclusive. Any variations, however, are noted.

4. *Ibid.*
5. Adams, *Kush* X (1962): 245–88. Use was also made of his unpublished *Handbook of Christian Nubian Pottery,* in which several important revisions are made to the earlier work.
6. Shinnie and Chittick, 1961.
7. Emery and Kirwan, 1935.

## Chapter Two:

# The Christian and X-Group Pottery

THE CERAMIC DESCRIPTIONS offered in this chapter are based solely upon materials collected in areas A–U, A–M, A–L, and N–U of the Classic Christian Townsite at Arminna West. Surface collections from other parts of the Arminna Plain and from area C–U are not included. The organization of the chapter follows the studies by Adams,[1] and additional comparative material has been drawn from Emery and Kirwan[2] and Shinnie.[3]

### I: Form Classes

Form is defined by Adams as "the overall shape and size of the vessel—qualities which are functionally deter-

mined within broad limits, but which are also strongly subject to stylistic modifications."[4] Eighteen form classes are distinguished. We shall discuss the occurrence of each of these in turn, reserving generalizations for the observations at the end of this chapter.

*Form Class "A": Saucers.*

Occurring only during Christian times, first in an imported ware from Egypt (ware 4: Samian red), later as an increasingly common native form, these "small, shallow bowls with curving or sloping sides" comprise 12.5% of the sherds and vessels found at Arminna West. Five sub-forms have been distinguished (fig. 22), one (A.3) a rare form occurring after A.D. 850, the remainder occurring with varying frequency from A.D. 600 onward. All forms have wide distribution except A.5, which is apparently restricted to Faras.

TABLE 2. Percentage Distribution of Form Class "A"
by Sub-class and Site Area, based upon a Sample of
498 Sherds and Vessels

| Sub-class | Surface | A–U | N–U | A–M | A–L | TOTAL[1] |
|---|---|---|---|---|---|---|
| A.1 | –.– | 11.4 | 9.6 | 1.8 | –.– | 22.8 |
| A.2 | 2.6 | 14.9 | 7.0 | 1.8 | –.– | 26.3 |
| A.3 | –.– | –.– | 2.6 | –.– | –.– | 2.6 |
| A.4 | 0.9 | 0.9 | 3.5 | –.– | –.– | 5.3 |
| A.5 | –.– | –.– | –.– | –.– | –.– | 0. |
| A.? | 8.8 | 28.1 | 1.8 | 4.3 | –.– | 43.0 |
| TOTAL[1] | 12.3 | 55.3 | 24.5 | 7.9 | 0. | 100.0 |

[1]Errors in totals are due to rounding.

In the Upper Building level, form "A" was found almost exclusively in rooms A–U–12a through A–U–12f (69% of form "A" sherds from A–U) and in N–U–Fore-

---

1. See Adams, *Kush* X (1962): 245–88, and his as yet unpublished *Handbook of Christian Nubian Pottery*. To avoid continuous and repetitious footnoting in this chapter, we have not cited every statement or quotation taken from these two works. It can be assumed, therefore, that all quotations which are not otherwise footnoted, and all general statements about forms and wares, are taken from Adams' studies. Our enormous debt to these works will be obvious even without repeated references. In all fairness to Dr. Adams, it should be noted that the *Handbook* was not intended for publication but was simply a tentative study designed to be used by archaeologists in the field. Several changes in the *Handbook* have already been made and will appear in the study of Nubian pottery now in preparation. I am deeply indebeted to Dr. Adams for allowing me to make use of materials in the *Handbook*.

2. Emery and Kirwan, 1935.

3. Shinnie and Chittick, 1961.

4. A more extensive discussion of this and other terms used in ceramic analysis can be found in Anna Shepard, 1956.

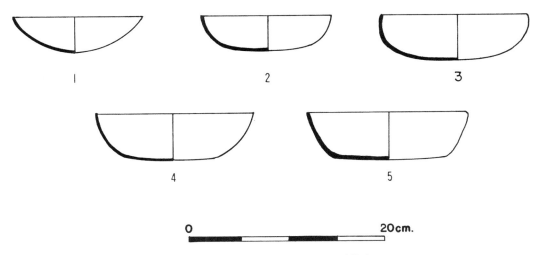

Fig. 22. Christian pottery form class "A": Saucers

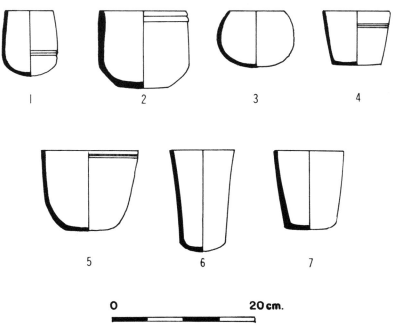

Fig. 23. Christian pottery form class "B": Cups

TABLE 3. Percentage Distribution of Decorative Styles in Form Class "A" by Form Sub-class, based upon a Sample of 354 Sherds and Vessels

| Style | A.1 | A.2 | A.3 | A.4 | A.5 | A.? | TOTAL[1] |
|---|---|---|---|---|---|---|---|
| a: Slipped, not painted | 9.8 | 4.9 | 0.8 | 3.2 | –.– | 13.0 | 31.7 |
| b: Rim band only | 2.4 | 2.4 | –.– | –.– | –.– | 6.5 | 11.3 |
| g: Classic Christian | 12.7 | 26.0 | –.– | 2.4 | –.– | 14.6 | 55.7 |
| s: Black and Red Bands | –.– | 1.6 | –.– | –.– | –.– | –.– | 1.6 |

[1]Errors in totals are due to rounding.

court (31% of those from N–U). In both these areas, over 50% of the "A" sherds were A.1 or A.2, 37% were A.? (unidentifiable sub-forms), and 8% were A.3 or A.4.

Seventy-one per cent of the form "A" sherds could be placed within Adams' style categories. Note the particularly high frequency of style "g," especially in sub-form A.2.

Table 4 lists those wares in which the occurrence of form class "A" has been noted by Adams and gives their frequency at Arminna West. Of interest is the almost complete absence of wares 2, 4, and 5, which Adams says are common in this form class, and the presence of ware 14, which he says is very rare. The physical characteristics of these wares will be discussed later in this chapter.

*Form Class "B": Cups.*

The seven sub-forms of form class "B" are described as "small, deep vessels with straight or steeply sloping sides." Forms B.1, B.3, and B.4 occur generally during X-Group and Early Christian times, while forms B.2, B.5, and B.7 are later forms.

Of those sherds from area A–U, 35% were from the Public Building, 33% from the room A–U–12 complex, and 32% from other rooms. In area N–U, 98% of the

TABLE 4. Percentage Distribution of Wares in Form Class "A" by Form Sub-class, based upon a Sample of 350 Sherds and Vessels

| Ware Number and Name | A.1 | A.2 | A.3 | A.4 | A.5 | A.? | TOTAL[1] |
|---|---|---|---|---|---|---|---|
| 2. Modified X-Group | –.– | –.– | –.– | –.– | –.– | –.– | 0. |
| 4. "Samian" Red | –.– | –.– | –.– | 1.1 | –.– | 1.1 | 2.1 |
| 5. Polished Red | –.– | –.– | –.– | –.– | –.– | 1.1 | 1.1 |
| 8. Red Crackled | –.– | –.– | –.– | –.– | –.– | –.– | 0. |
| 12. Transitional White | 7.3 | 2.0 | –.– | –.– | –.– | 9.4 | 18.8 |
| 14. Early Classic Christian | –.– | –.– | –.– | –.– | –.– | 2.0 | 2.0 |
| 15. Classic Christian White | 12.5 | 23.6 | –.– | 3.1 | –.– | 20.4 | 59.6 |
| 16. Classic Christian Yellow | 4.2 | 4.2 | –.– | 1.1 | –.– | 6.2 | 15.6 |
| 18. Plain Soft White | –.– | –.– | –.– | –.– | –.– | –.– | 0. |
| 19. Hard White | –.– | –.– | –.– | –.– | –.– | –.– | 0. |
| 20. Polished Yellow | –.– | –.– | –.– | –.– | –.– | 1.1 | 1.1 |

[1]Errors in totals are due to rounding.

sherds were from N–U–Forecourt. Sherds from the Middle Building level (A–M) were from A–M–6 and A–M–11 exclusively.

TABLE 5. Percentage Distribution of Form Class "B" by Sub-class and Site Area, based upon a Sample of 200 Sherds and Vessels

| Sub-class | Surface | A–U | N–U | A–M | A–L | TOTAL[1] |
|---|---|---|---|---|---|---|
| B.1 | –.– | –.– | 10.2 | 18.4 | –.– | 28.6 |
| B.2 | –.– | 38.8 | 2.1 | 2.1 | –.– | 42.9 |
| B.3 | –.– | –.– | –.– | –.– | –.– | 0. |
| B.4 | 2.1 | –.– | 2.1 | 2.1 | –.– | 6.2 |
| B.5 | –.– | –.– | 2.1 | –.– | –.– | 2.1 |
| B.6 | –.– | –.– | –.– | –.– | –.– | 0. |
| B.7 | –.– | –.– | –.– | –.– | –.– | 0. |
| B.? | –.– | 18.4 | 2.1 | –.– | –.– | 20.4 |
| TOTAL[1] | 2.1 | 57.1 | 18.5 | 22.5 | –.– | 100.0 |

[1]Errors in totals are due to rounding.

Twenty-six per cent of form "B" sherds were of style "a," "slipped, not decorated." Forms B.1 and B.4 were decorated with either a simple rim band (style "b") or with parallel body grooves (relief decoration PBG). Forms B.2 and B.? were decorated in styles "c" and "g."

Table 6 lists those wares in which form class "B" is known to occur. Those wares preceded by an asterisk are examples which Adams does not include in his list of form class "B" wares but which occur with fair frequency at Arminna West. These non-Adams examples will be described in detail later in this chapter.

*Form Class "C": Plain Bowls.*

Fourteen sub-forms have been distinguished, of which two (C.7 and C.9) occur in X-Group and Early Christian times. All forms except C.5, C.7, C.9, and C.10 appear to be rare at all times, and even these four exceptions diminish in frequency during later periods.

Of those form class "C" sherds from area A–U almost 40% were sub-form C.4, and of these, 46% were from the room 12 complex, 20% from the Public Building, and 34% were from rooms A–U–2 and A–U–3. In area N–U, all but five of the "C" sherds were from N–U–Forecourt. All C.5 sherds in A–U came either from A–U–3 or A–U–12c.

Sixty-two per cent of the sherds were style "a," "slipped, not painted." The remainder were decorated in styles "b," "f," or "g," or with incised rim grooves. Most of the decorated sherds are of form C.2 or C.5. (Examples of incised decoration are shown in fig. 43.)

TABLE 7. Percentage Distribution of Form Class "C" by Sub-class and Site Area, based upon a Sample of 235 Sherds and Vessels

| Sub-class | Surface | A–U | N–U | A–M | A–L | TOTAL[1] |
|---|---|---|---|---|---|---|
| C.1 | –.– | 1.6 | 1.6 | –.– | –.– | 3.1 |
| C.2 | –.– | –.– | 1.6 | 3.2 | –.– | 4.8 |
| C.3 | –.– | –.– | –.– | –.– | –.– | 0. |
| C.4 | –.– | 23.8 | 6.3 | 1.6 | –.– | 31.7 |
| C.5 | 1.6 | 9.5 | 1.6 | –.– | –.– | 12.7 |
| C.6 | 1.6 | –.– | –.– | –.– | –.– | 1.6 |
| C.7 | –.– | –.– | 1.6 | 1.6 | –.– | 3.2 |
| C.8 | –.– | –.– | –.– | –.– | –.– | 0. |
| C.9 | –.– | –.– | –.– | 4.8 | –.– | 4.8 |
| C.10 | –.– | 1.6 | 3.2 | –.– | –.– | 4.8 |
| C.11 | –.– | –.– | –.– | –.– | –.– | 0. |
| C.12 | –.– | 1.6 | –.– | –.– | –.– | 1.6 |
| C.13 | –.– | –.– | –.– | –.– | –.– | 0. |
| C.14 | –.– | –.– | –.– | –.– | –.– | 0. |
| C.? | 3.2 | 22.2 | 3.2 | 3.2 | –.– | 31.7 |
| TOTAL[1] | 6.3 | 60.3 | 19.0 | 14.3 | 0. | 100.0 |

[1]Errors in totals are due to rounding.

The frequency of occurrence of the ten wares in which form class "C" is known to occur is shown in Table 8. Wares marked by an asterisk, here Classic Christian White, have not been noted by Adams to occur in this form class.

Fifteen sherds or whole vessels, five of which are shown in fig. 24, are by association of Christian or X-Group date and may belong in form class "C," although they are not included in Adams' classification. The specimens are of ware 12 or 16.

TABLE 6. Percentage Distribution of Wares in Form Class "B" by Form Sub-class, based upon a Sample of 175 Sherds and Vessels. (No examples of Sub-forms B.6 or B.7.)

| Ware Number and Name | B.1 | B.2 | B.3 | B.4 | B.5 | B.? | TOTAL[1] |
|---|---|---|---|---|---|---|---|
| 1. Classic X-Group | 6.5 | –.– | –.– | –.– | –.– | 2.2 | 8.7 |
| 2. Modified X-Group | 8.7 | –.– | –.– | 4.3 | –.– | 2.2 | 15.2 |
| 6. Transitional Soft Red | –.– | –.– | –.– | –.– | –.– | –.– | 0. |
| 9. Micaceous Red | –.– | –.– | –.– | –.– | –.– | –.– | 0. |
| 11. Orange/White | –.– | –.– | –.– | –.– | –.– | –.– | 0. |
| 12. Transitional White | –.– | 10.9 | 2.2 | –.– | –.– | 13.0 | 26.1 |
| 16. Classic Christian Yellow | 6.5 | 8.7 | –.– | –.– | –.– | 4.3 | 19.6 |
| *10. *X-Group White | 2.2 | 2.2 | –.– | –.– | 4.3 | 8.7 | 17.4 |
| *15. *Classic Christian White | 2.2 | 8.7 | –.– | –.– | –.– | 2.2 | 13.0 |

[1]Errors in totals are due to rounding.
*Asterisks mark ware-form combinations not noted by Adams.

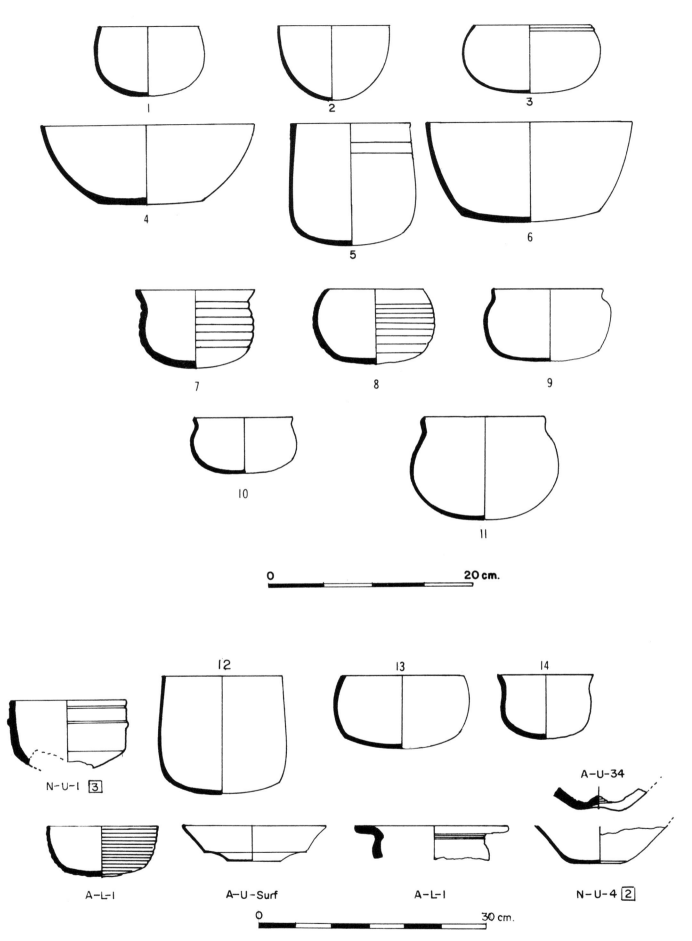

0          20 cm.

12          13          14

N-U-1 3

A-U-34

A-L-1          A-U-Surf          A-L-1          N-U-4 2

0                              30 cm.

Fig. 24. Christian pottery form class "C": Bowls

TABLE 8. Percentage Distribution of Wares in Form Class "C" by Form Sub-class,
based upon a Sample of 170 Sherds and Vessels.
(No examples of Sub-forms C.3, C.8, C.11, C.13, or C.14.)

| Ware Number and Name | C.1 | C.2 | C.4 | C.5 | C.6 | C.7 | C.9 | C.10 | C.12 | C.? | TOTAL[1] |
|---|---|---|---|---|---|---|---|---|---|---|---|
| 2. Modified X-Group | –.– | –.– | 6.1 | –.– | –.– | –.– | –.– | –.– | –.– | –.– | 6.1 |
| 3. Transitional Red-Orange | –.– | –.– | 10.2 | –.– | –.– | –.– | –.– | 2.0 | –.– | 6.1 | 18.4 |
| 6. Transitional Soft Red | –.– | –.– | –.– | –.– | –.– | –.– | –.– | –.– | –.– | –.– | 0. |
| 9. Micaceous Red | –.– | –.– | –.– | –.– | –.– | –.– | –.– | –.– | –.– | –.– | 0. |
| 7. Classic Christian Red | –.– | –.– | 10.2 | –.– | –.– | –.– | –.– | –.– | –.– | 2.0 | 12.3 |
| 12. Transitional White | –.– | –.– | –.– | 4.1 | –.– | 4.1 | –.– | 4.1 | –.– | 6.1 | 18.4 |
| 16. Classic Christian Yellow | 2.0 | 2.0 | –.– | 4.1 | 8.2 | 2.0 | –.– | –.– | 2.0 | 10.2 | 30.6 |
| 18. Plain Soft White | –.– | –.– | –.– | –.– | –.– | –.– | –.– | –.– | –.– | –.– | 0. |
| 19. Hard White | –.– | –.– | –.– | –.– | –.– | –.– | –.– | –.– | –.– | 6.1 | 6.1 |
| 20. Polished Yellow | –.– | –.– | –.– | –.– | –.– | –.– | –.– | –.– | –.– | –.– | 0. |
| 27. Coarse Domestic | –.– | –.– | –.– | –.– | –.– | –.– | –.– | –.– | –.– | –.– | 0. |
| *15. *Classic Christian White | –.– | –.– | –.– | 2.0 | 2.0 | –.– | –.– | –.– | –.– | 4.1 | 8.2 |

[1]Errors in totals are due to rounding.
*Asterisk marks ware-form combination not noted by Adams.

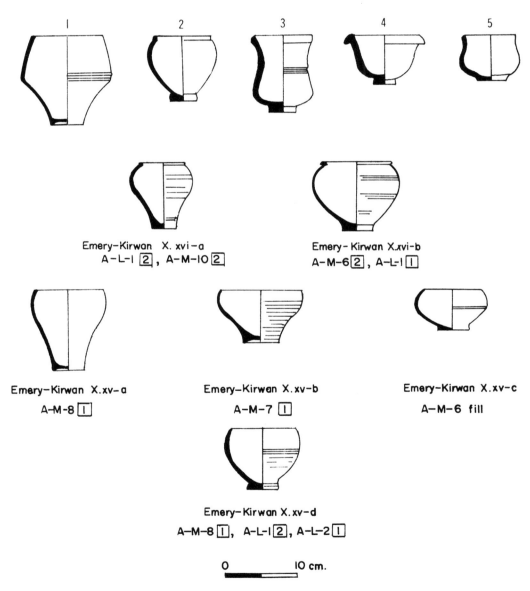

Fig. 25. Christian pottery form class "D": Goblets

41

*Form Class "D": Goblets* (pl. Xa).

The five sub-forms of form class "D" are found only prior to about A.D. 600, i.e., only during the X-Group period. Sub-forms D.1 and D.2 are common, while sub-forms D.3, D.4, and D.5 are at all times rare.

TABLE 9. Percentage Distribution of Form Class "D" by Sub-class and Site Area, based upon a Sample of 750 Sherds and Vessels

| Sub-class | Surface | A–U | N–U | A–M | A–L | TOTAL[1] |
|---|---|---|---|---|---|---|
| D.1 | 0.9 | 2.0 | –.– | 24.3 | 4.5 | 31.7 |
| D.2 | –.– | 9.9 | 0.5 | 36.6 | 5.0 | 51.9 |
| D.3 | –.– | –.– | –.– | –.– | –.– | 0. |
| D.4 | –.– | –.– | –.– | –.– | –.– | 0. |
| D.5 | –.– | –.– | –.– | –.– | –.– | 0. |
| D.? | –.– | 0.9 | –.– | 14.4 | 0.9 | 16.3 |
| TOTAL[1] | 0.9 | 12.8 | 0.5 | 75.4 | 10.4 | 100.0 |

[1]Errors in totals are due to rounding.

Finds of form D.1 in the Middle Building level (A–M) were from rooms A–M–6, A–M–9, and A–M–11 in over 80% of the cases. Form D.2 in the Middle Building level was largely from A–M–6 (30%), A–M–11 (12%), A–M–8 (16%), and A–M–3 (10%). (See pl. Xa for selected A–M examples.)

In sub-form D.2, 95% of the sherds were of style "a," slipped but not decorated. The remainder had parallel body grooves, corrugation, or a style c-1 rim band. The few decorated D.1 sherds were either of style d-1 or d-4 pendant designs, or d-1 and d-3 body splash patterns.

TABLE 10. Percentage Distribution of Wares in Form Class "D" by Form Sub-class, based upon a Sample of 500 Sherds and Vessels

| Ware Number and Name | D.1 | D.2 | D.3 | D.4 | D.5 | D.? | TOTAL[1] |
|---|---|---|---|---|---|---|---|
| 1. Classic X-Group | 28.3 | 37.1 | –.– | –.– | –.– | –.– | 65.4 |
| *2. *Modified X-Group | 10.1 | 26.4 | –.– | –.– | –.– | –.– | 36.5 |

[1]Errors in totals are due to rounding.
*Asterisk marks ware-form combination not noted by Adams.

Adams notes the occurrence of form class "D" only in ware 1. Numerous examples of form D in ware 2 can be seen at Arminna, however, and would suggest that an X-Group date for form class "D" should be modified to include at least the early Transitional Period.

Several goblets illustrated by Emery and Kirwan,[5] though certainly of Adams' form class "D," do not appear in his classification.

Thirteen examples of what Emery and Kirwan designate as form X.xvi-a were found at Arminna, ten of them in level 2 of room A–L–1, three in level 2 of room A–M–10. All sherds were of fine to medium texture,

5. Emery and Kirwan, 1935: I, 516 and II, pl. 40.

well-fired, with quartz sand and mica temper, and were of medium hardness. Paste was either 5 YR 6/4 or 10 R 6/6, slip either 10 R 7/4 (two examples) or 10 R 5/4 (eleven examples). Only two sherds were decorated and these were lightly ribbed.

Seven examples of X.xvi-b were recovered, four from A–M–6 level 2, and three from A–L–1 level 1. All were well-fired, of medium texture, medium hardness, and all had quartz sand temper. Paste color was 10 R 6/6 or 5 YR 6/4; slip in all cases was 10 R 5/4. Three sherds were lightly corrugated.

Thirteen examples of X.xv forms were found, three X.xv-a, one X.xv-b, and six X.xv-d. All examples of X.xv-d were decorated with examples of Adams' style d-3 body covering pattern. Sherds of forms –a, and –b were undecorated. All sherds had quartz sand and mica temper, were well-fired and of medium texture with a hardness of +6.5. Paste was generally either 10 R 6/6 or 5 YR 7/4; slip was either 10 R 6/6 or 10 R 5/4.

Emery and Kirwan assign all sherds of these forms to the X-Group period.

TABLE 11. Percentage Distribution of Form Class "E" by Sub-class and Site Area, based upon a Sample of 675 Sherds and Vessels

| Sub-class | Surface | A–U | N–U | A–M | A–L | TOTAL[1] |
|---|---|---|---|---|---|---|
| E.1 | –.– | 1.0 | –.– | –.– | –.– | 1.0 |
| E.2 | –.– | 1.0 | –.– | –.– | –.– | 1.0 |
| E.3 | 0.5 | 1.5 | –.– | 0.5 | –.– | 2.6 |
| E.4 | 5.6 | 24.5 | 12.8 | 1.0 | –.– | 43.9 |
| E.5 | –.– | 0.5 | 0.5 | 0.5 | –.– | 1.5 |
| E.6 | –.– | 1.0 | 1.0 | –.– | –.– | 2.0 |
| E.7 | –.– | –.– | –.– | –.– | –.– | 0. |
| E.8 | –.– | –.– | –.– | 0.5 | –.– | 0.5 |
| E.9 | –.– | 2.6 | 0.5 | –.– | –.– | 3.1 |
| E.10 | –.– | –.– | –.– | –.– | –.– | 0. |
| E.11 | –.– | –.– | –.– | –.– | –.– | 0. |
| E.12 | –.– | –.– | –.– | –.– | –.– | 0. |
| E.13 | –.– | –.– | –.– | –.– | –.– | 0. |
| E.14 | –.– | –.– | –.– | –.– | –.– | 0. |
| E.15 | –.– | –.– | –.– | 0.5 | –.– | 0.5 |
| E.? | 1.0 | 27.5 | 12.8 | 2.6 | –.– | 43.9 |
| TOTAL[1] | 7.1 | 59.7 | 27.5 | 5.6 | –.– | 100.0 |

[1]Errors in totals are due to rounding.

*Form Class "E": Footed Bowls.*

Fifteen sub-forms of form class "E" have been distinguished. They are moderately common during X-Group times and abundant during the Christian period. Most of the sub-forms occur between A.D. 650 and 850, while forms E.3, E.8, E.10, and E.15 are found prior to that time, and forms E.11, E.12, and E.14 occur only after A.D. 1100.

In the Upper Building level of area A, form E.4 was found almost exclusively in rooms A–U–3, the Public Building, and the A–U–12 complex. In area N–U, the

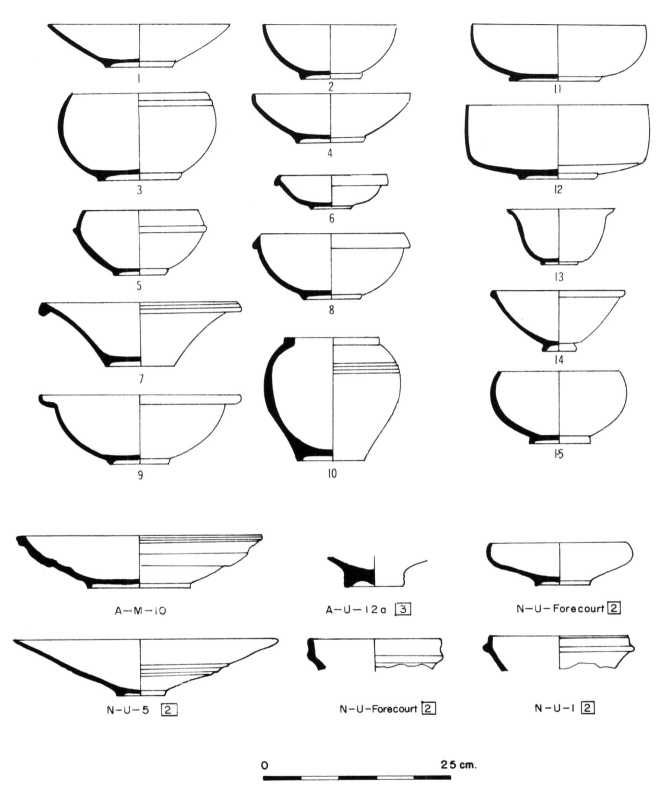

1
2
3
4
5
6
7
8
9
10
11
12
13
14
15

A—M—10

A—U—12a ③

N—U—Forecourt ②

N—U—5 ②

N—U—Forecourt ②

N—U—1 ②

0                    25 cm.

Fig. 26. Christian pottery form class "E": Footed Bowls

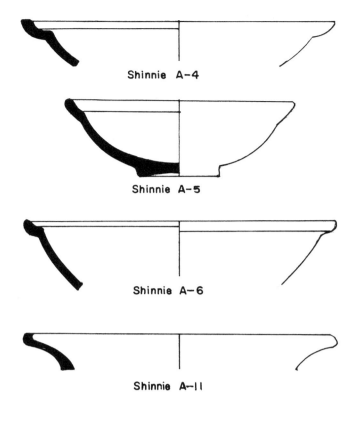

Shinnie A-4

Shinnie A-5

Shinnie A-6

Shinnie A-11

0    5    10 cm.

Fig. 27. Christian pottery form class "E": Variations
(after Shinnie, and Chittick, *Ghazali,* fig. 6)

majority of all form "E" sherds came from N–U–Forecourt, level 2.

Styles were most frequently "a," slipped and not decorated, or "b," rim band only. There are, however, some examples of incised rim grooves and a few examples of style "g" motifs.

Four examples of P. L. Shinnie's type A.6 were found, two in N–U–Forecourt level 2, two in room A–M–7 level 1. They most closely resemble his types A.4, A.6, A.5, and A.11 and can readily be placed within Adams' form class "E."[6]

Several other vessels which resemble none of the examples in Adams' or Shinnie's classifications are shown in figure 26. They are of wares 12 or 16.

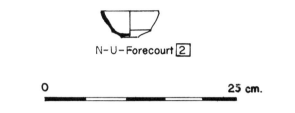

N–U–Forecourt 2

0                              25 cm.

Fig. 28. Christian pottery form class "F": Miniature Bowls

*Form Class "F": Miniature Bowls.*

Although described as common from A.D. 600 to 750, the six sub-forms of miniature bowls described by Adams do not occur at Arminna West. Only one miniature bowl, a non-Adams form, was found on the site, in level 2 of N–U–Forecourt.

6.  Shinnie and Chittick, 1961: 32 and fig. 6.

TABLE 12. Percentage Distribution of Wares in Form Class "E" by Form Sub-class,
based upon a Sample of 450 Sherds and Vessels.
(No examples of Sub-forms E.7, E.10, E.11, E.12, E.13, or E.14.)

| Ware Number and Name | E.1 | E.2 | E.3 | E.4 | E.5 | E.6 | E.8 | E.9 | E.15 | E.? | TOTAL |
|---|---|---|---|---|---|---|---|---|---|---|---|
| 1.  Classic X-Group | –.– | –.– | –.– | –.– | –.– | –.– | –.– | –.– | 0.7 | 1.4 | 2.1 |
| 2.  Modified X-Group | –.– | –.– | –.– | –.– | –.– | –.– | –.– | –.– | –.– | 0.7 | 0.7 |
| 3.  Transitional Red-Orange | –.– | –.– | –.– | –.– | –.– | –.– | –.– | –.– | –.– | 2.1 | 2.1 |
| 4.  "Samian" Red | –.– | –.– | –.– | –.– | –.– | 0.7 | 0.7 | –.– | –.– | 2.1 | 3.5 |
| 5.  Polished Red | –.– | –.– | –.– | 1.4 | –.– | 0.7 | –.– | –.– | –.– | 2.1 | 4.2 |
| 6.  Transitional Soft Red | –.– | –.– | 1.4 | –.– | –.– | –.– | –.– | –.– | –.– | –.– | 1.4 |
| 8.  Red Crackled | –.– | –.– | –.– | –.– | –.– | –.– | –.– | –.– | –.– | –.– | 0. |
| 9.  Micaceous Red | –.– | –.– | –.– | –.– | –.– | –.– | –.– | –.– | –.– | –.– | 0. |
| 10.  X-Group White | –.– | –.– | –.– | 0.7 | –.– | –.– | –.– | –.– | –.– | 2.1 | 2.8 |
| 11.  Orange/White | –.– | –.– | –.– | –.– | 0.7 | –.– | –.– | –.– | –.– | –.– | 0.7 |
| 12.  Transitional White | 0.7 | –.– | 0.7 | 4.2 | –.– | –.– | –.– | –.– | –.– | 7.5 | 13.2 |
| 13.  "Samian" Cream | –.– | –.– | –.– | 0.7 | –.– | 0.7 | –.– | –.– | –.– | –.– | 1.4 |
| 15.  Classic Christian White | –.– | –.– | –.– | 9.9 | –.– | –.– | –.– | –.– | –.– | 4.2 | 14.0 |
| 16.  Classic Christian Yellow | –.– | –.– | 0.7 | 21.1 | 0.7 | –.– | –.– | 4.2 | –.– | 16.9 | 43.5 |
| 18.  Plain Soft White | –.– | –.– | –.– | –.– | –.– | –.– | –.– | –.– | –.– | –.– | 0. |
| 19.  Hard White | –.– | –.– | –.– | –.– | –.– | –.– | –.– | –.– | –.– | –.– | 0. |
| 20.  Polished Yellow | –.– | –.– | –.– | –.– | –.– | –.– | –.– | –.– | –.– | 2.8 | 2.8 |
| *7.  *Classic Christian Red | –.– | –.– | 0.7 | 2.1 | 0.7 | –.– | –.– | –.– | –.– | 3.5 | 7.0 |

*Asterisk marks ware-form combination not noted by Adams.

*Form Class "G": Vases.*

With the exception of G.13, which first appears *ca.* A.D. 500, and G.1, G.3, and G.4, which appear around A.D. 650, none of the thirteen sub-forms of class "G" occur prior to A.D. 850. Most of the forms are described as rare, although G.12 apparently occurs in abundance and G.3, G.4, and G.5 occur with fair frequency after A.D. 1100.

Of those sherds from area A–U, the vast majority (*ca.*

80%) were from the room A–U–12 complex. The remainder were from the Public Building, A–U–2, and A–U–3. In area N–U, the sherds were from N–U–Forecourt and N–U–8.

Ninety-four per cent of the form class "G" sherds were decorated and were with but one exception (an "f-2" body band on a G.4 sherd) of style "g."

Nine forms not included by Adams but which would seem most easily included in his form class "G" are shown

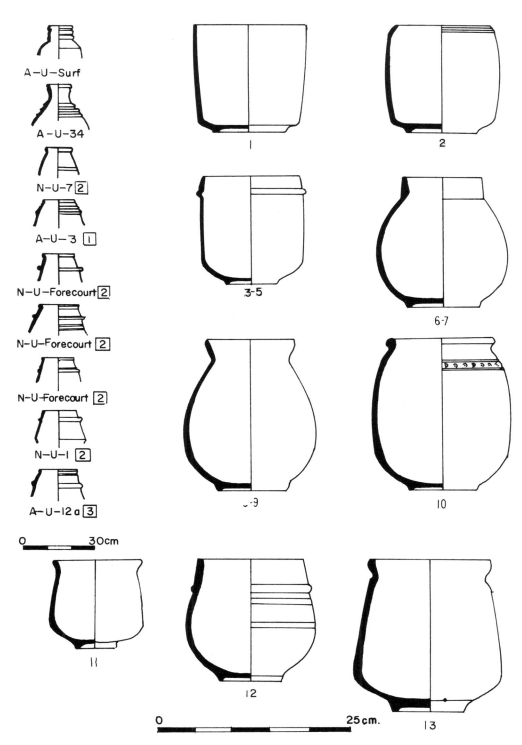

Fig. 29. Christian pottery form class "G": Vases

45

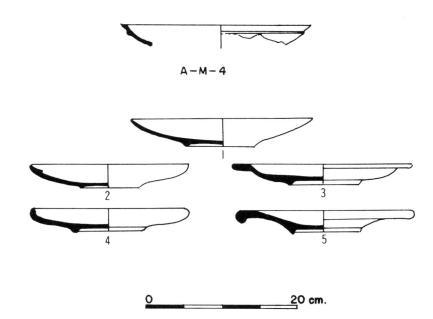

A–M–4

0          20 cm.

Fig. 30. Christian pottery form class "H": Plates

in fig. 29. Associated materials would suggest that they are all of Classic or Late Christian date. (But for their large size, the two forms from A–U–surface and A–U–34 could almost be included in his form class "N": Bottles.) All specimens appear to be of ware 7.

TABLE 13. Percentage Distribution of Form Class "G" by Sub-class and Site Area, based upon a Sample of 275 Sherds and Vessels. (No examples of Sub-forms G.7, G.8, G.9, G.10, G.11, G.12, or G.13.)

| Sub-Class | Surface | A–U | N–U | A–M | A–L | TOTAL[1] |
|---|---|---|---|---|---|---|
| G.1 | –.– | 3.7 | –.– | –.– | –.– | 3.7 |
| G.2 | –.– | –.– | –.– | –.– | –.– | 0. |
| G.3 | 1.2 | 18.3 | 4.9 | –.– | –.– | 24.4 |
| G.4 | –.– | 17.1 | 1.2 | –.– | –.– | 18.3 |
| G.5 | –.– | 4.9 | 1.2 | –.– | –.– | 6.1 |
| G.6 | –.– | 2.4 | –.– | –.– | –.– | 2.4 |
| G.? | 7.3 | 30.5 | 7.3 | –.– | –.– | 45.1 |
| TOTAL[1] | 8.5 | 76.8 | 14.7 | 0. | 0. | 100.0 |

[1]Errors in totals are due to rounding.

*Form Class "H": Plates.*

Adams states that examples of form class "H" are "very rare and found only in trade pieces in the Christian period." Of the six forms he describes, none occur prior to A.D. 600, and two, H.2 and H.5, occur only between A.D. 600 and 750.

At Arminna West, only twenty-five examples were found, one from room A–U–5 level 1, seven from level 2 of N–U–Forecourt, the remainder from the A–U–12 complex. Five of these were form H.2, one was H.3, one H.4, five H.5; the remainder were H.?.

The form class is said to occur in wares 5, 11, 13, and 16. At Arminna West, four examples of ware 5: Polished Red were found. The remainder were ware 16: Classic Christian Yellow. There were no examples of wares 11: Orange/White or 13: "Samian" Cream.

Only five sherds were decorated, one with an emblem centerpiece (fig. 44b), the other with style "b" rim bands.

One specimen from room A–M–4 (fig. 30) may also be a form class "H" type.

TABLE 14. Percentage Distribution of Wares in Form Class "G" by Form Sub-class,
based upon a Sample of 210 Sherds and Vessels.
(No examples of Sub-forms G.7, G.8, G.9, G.10, G.11, G.12, or G.13.)

| Ware Number and Name | G.1 | G.2 | G.3 | G.4 | G.5 | G.6 | G.? | TOTAL[1] |
|---|---|---|---|---|---|---|---|---|
| 7. Classic Christian Red | –.– | –.– | 2.0 | 2.0 | –.– | –.– | –.– | 4.0 |
| 14. Early Classic Christian | 2.0 | –.– | –.– | –.– | 2.0 | –.– | 2.0 | 6.0 |
| 16. Classic Christian Yellow | 2.0 | –.– | 10.0 | 20.0 | 6.0 | –.– | 22.0 | 60.0 |
| 17. Christian Heavy Decorated | –.– | –.– | 8.0 | 2.0 | –.– | 2.0 | 8.0 | 20.0 |
| *12. *Transitional White | –.– | –.– | –.– | 6.0 | –.– | –.– | 4.0 | 10.0 |

[1]Errors in totals are due to rounding.
*Asterisk marks ware-form combination not noted by Adams.

*Form Class "J": Dokas.*

Two sub-forms are recognized, one flat and one concave. Both occur abundantly throughout the X-Group and Christian periods.

At Arminna West, only six examples were found, all J.1, one from A–U–2, the remainder from N–U–Forecourt. All were of ware 27: Coarse Domestic ware.

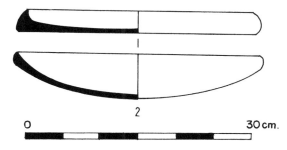

Fig. 31. Christian pottery form class "J": *Dokas*

*Form Class "K": Storage Jars.*

Adams distinguishes two sub-forms, "necked" and "neckless," the latter occurring after A.D. 400, the former after A.D. 600 (although there is some uncertainty about their presence in X-Group contexts).

At Arminna West, thirty examples were found, all form K.1. Of these, three are from N–U–Forecourt, one is from A–U–34, and the remainder are from levels 2 and 3 of the A–U–12 complex. Although their occurrence is noted in wares 3, 7, 10, 12, 21, and 25, all examples from Arminna are of ware 25: Christian Red Utility. Most examples are decorated with either wavy body grooves or parallel body grooves.

One unusual necked form from N–U–Forecourt is shown in fig. 32.

*Form Class "L": Neckless Pots.*

Six sub-forms, all but two of which (L.4: A.D. 400–600; L.6: A.D. 600–750) occur throughout X-Group and Christian times, have been distinguished. No form except L.1 is particularly common prior to A.D. 1000, after which time L.5 is the most frequently found.

At Arminna West, thirty examples of form class "L" were found, ten of which were L.2 (N–U–Forecourt and area A–M), nine L.3 (all surface finds), six L.1 (area A–M and A–U–9), one L.5 (A–M–11) and four L.? (A–U–12 complex).

Adams states that form class "L" is found in wares 25, 26, and 27. At Arminna eight examples of ware 25 were found, six of ware 27; the remainder were unidentifiable.

Most examples were undecorated. Of eight decorated specimens, three were style "b": simple rim bands, four were collar bands of style "f," and one was corrugated and resembled Emery-Kirwan's form X.xi-a.[7]

Two forms which may belong in this form class are shown in fig. 33.

*Form Class "M": Necked Bottles.*

Specimens of this form class occur primarily in X-Group and Early Christian times, although forms M.3, M.4, M.5, M.7, and M.8 are found throughout the Classic and Late Christian periods as well. Of the eight sub-forms distinguished by Adams, only forms M.1, M.2, and M.7 appear to be common at any time, and forms M.1, M.2, and M.6 are restricted in occurrence to *ca.* A.D. 550–750.

Twenty-five examples were found at Arminna West, eighteen of them M.4, five of them M.1, and two M.2. Examples were from A–U–6, the A–U–12 complex, N–U–Forecourt, A–M–4, and A–M–9.

7. Emery and Kirwan, 1935: I, 515 and II, pl. 39.

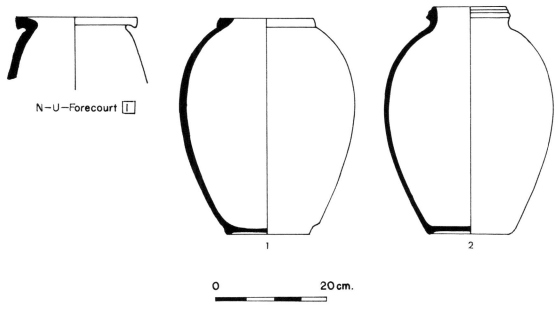

Fig. 32. Christian pottery form class "K": Storage Jars

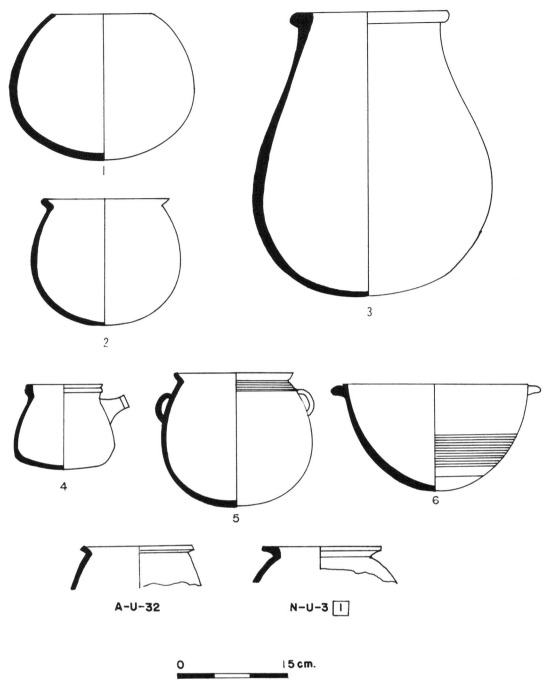

Fig. 33. Christian pottery form class "L": Neckless Pots

Only three of the specimens were decorated: one M.1 form had a rim band with style RG incisions, another had a g-5 interior collar band, and one M.2 form had a g-1 suspended wall frieze.

Adams notes the occurrence of this form in wares 1, 10, 19, 25, 26, and 27. At Arminna, 60% of the examples were ware 27, 40% ware 25.

Three non-Adams forms are shown in fig. 34, all of ware 27. Their inclusion in this form class is tentative.

*Form Class "N": Bottles.*

Although abundant in X-Group times, examples of this form become increasingly rare during the Christian period. Ten sub-forms are distinguished. Forms N.1 and N.6 occur only prior to A.D. 550; forms N.4 and N.9 only after A.D. 850. N.8 occurs after A.D. 600, while the remainder of the forms are found throughout the X-Group and Christian periods. Only forms N.2, N.4, and N.6 are described as common.

48

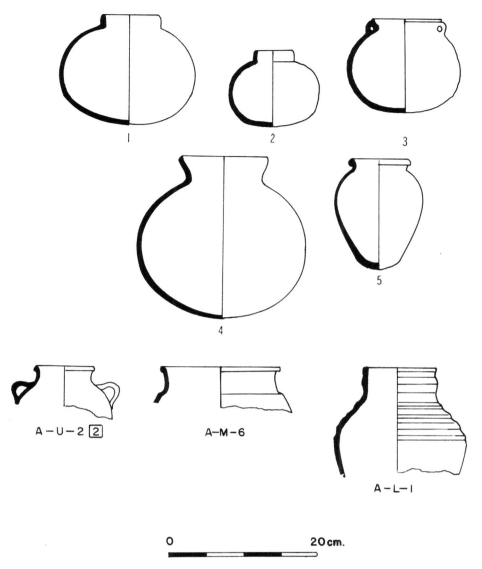

Fig. 34. Christian pottery form class "M": Necked Pots

At Arminna West, of forty-four examples of this form class, twenty are of form N.2, ten are N.1, one is N.3, one N.4, and twelve are N.?.

Only 30% of the specimens are decorated, all in style "f." The remainder are style "a," slipped and not decorated.

Adams states that this form class occurs in wares 1, 3, 25, and 27. At Arminna, 60% are of ware 25, 30% are ware 27, and 10% are unknown. All examples of ware 25 are of medium texture, well-fired, of medium hardness, with quartz sand temper, occasionally with some straw levigation. Paste color is either 5 YR 6/4 or 10 R 6/6; slip is generally 10 R 6/2.

Five non-Adams forms, all of ware 25, are shown in fig. 35.

*Form Class "P": Amphorae.*

Adams remarks that these are "found only in imported wares until late Christian times" and that they are "especially valuable for dating because of Egyptian origin." He distinguishes five sub-forms, of which P.3 and P.5 occur only before A.D. 550, P.2 before A.D. 750, and P.4 during the entire Christian period. P.1 occurs between A.D. 500 and 750 and was possibly re-introduced after A.D. 1100.

Specimens from area A–U are exclusively from rooms A–U–4, A–U–5, and A–U–12c. Finds from area A–M

TABLE 15. Percentage Distribution of Form Class "P" by Sub-class and Site Area, based upon a Sample of 194 Sherds and Vessels

| Sub-class | Surface | A–U | N–U | A–M | A–L | TOTAL[1] |
|---|---|---|---|---|---|---|
| P.1 | –.– | 3.5 | –.– | 31.4 | –.– | 35.0 |
| P.2 | –.– | –.– | –.– | 3.5 | –.– | 3.5 |
| P.3 | –.– | 3.5 | –.– | 3.5 | –.– | 7.0 |
| P.4 | –.– | 3.5 | 1.8 | –.– | –.– | 5.3 |
| P.5 | –.– | –.– | –.– | –.– | –.– | 0. |
| P.? | –.– | 26.3 | 5.3 | 15.8 | 1.8 | 49.1 |
| TOTAL[1] | 0. | 36.8 | 7.1 | 54.4 | 1.8 | 100.0 |

[1]Errors in totals are due to rounding.

49

are from A–M–4, A–M–6, A–M–7, and A–M–9.

Style RB (ribbing) occurs on over 60% of all specimens. The remainder are merely slipped.

Form Class "P" is said to occur in wares 22, 23, 24, and 25. At Arminna 31% of the specimens were of ware 22, 7% in ware 24, 9% in ware 25, and 2% in ware 23. Identifiable P.1 forms were of ware 22 and this ware occurs in no other sub-form. This is in keeping with Adams' remark that the ware "is identified with certainty only in amphorae of Form P1." The ware is of Adams' fabric IV, and all Arminna specimens fall well within his description: fine texture, hard, often only moderately well-fired, paste usually 10 R 7/4 or 5 YR 8/4, slip usually 10 R 6/6 or 5 YR 8/4.

Two non-Adams forms, both of ware 22, are shown in fig. 36 (see also pl. Xd).

*Form Class "Q": Pilgrim Bottles.*

Only four examples were found at Arminna, all from area A–U. They fit Adams' description of the form and all occurred in ware 17, fabric III, and were decorated in styles "c" and "g." Adams notes that the form is rare prior to A.D. 850 but abundant after A.D. 1100 (see pl. Xe).

*Form Class "R": Qadus.*

There is only one form common throughout X-Group and Christian times, found in wares 21, and 25, fabrics II and III, styles "a" and "f."

Thirty-five examples were found at Arminna West. Nine examples were from area A–M (rooms A–M–6, A–M–8, and A–M–9) and were all of ware 21; four were from area A–L level 1, and were also of ware 21; the remainder were from area A–U, rooms A–U–3, A–U–12a–f, and A–U–35, and were exclusively ware 25.

*Form Class "S": Basins.*

The form class is found in four sub-forms, three of which occur throughout X-Group and Christian times, one of which (S.4) is found only after A.D. 1200 and even then only rarely. The form is described as consisting of "large, heavy vessels with nearly straight sides and flat bottoms."

Twelve examples were found at Arminna West, all of form S.2, all ware 25, and all but two (which were style "b") decorated by punching or incising (fig. 43).

*Form Class "T": Pipes.*

No examples.

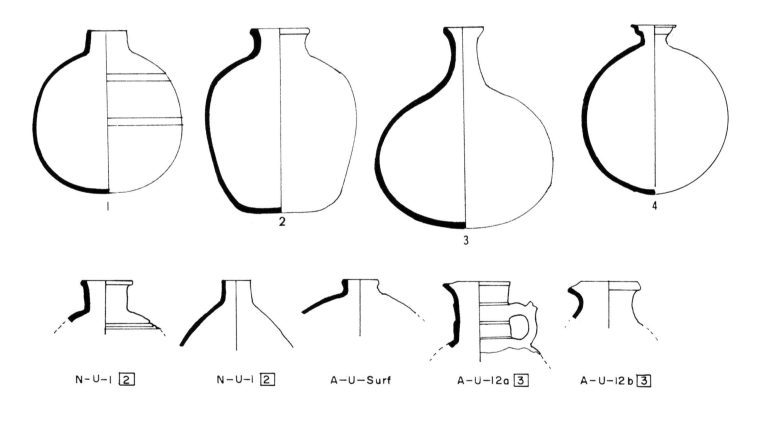

N–U–1 [2]          N–U–1 [2]          A–U–Surf          A–U–12a [3]          A–U–12b [3]

0                    20 cm.

Fig. 35. Christian pottery form class "N": Bottles

*Other.*

Four examples of spouted vessels similar to that shown by Emery and Kirwan in their fig. X.xiii-a[8] were found at Arminna West, all from levels 2 and 3 of room A–M–6. One of these is shown in fig. 39. In all four cases, the vessels were well-fired, of fine texture and medium hardness, and had quartz sand and black temper. Paste was either 5 YR 5/4 or 5 YR 6/4, slip either 10 R 5/4 or 10 R 6/4. Emery and Kirwan assign to these vessels an X-Group date.

A few examples of sherds which, at least in terms of form, fit the typology of P. L. Shinnie[9] but cannot be

8. *Ibid.*
9. Shinnie and Chittick, 1961: 33, 34, and figs. 7, 8, 10, 16, 17, 18.

placed in Adams' classification, were found at Arminna West.

One example of his type B (B.1) was found in room N–U–5 level 2 (fig. 39). Three examples of C.7 came from N–U–Forecourt level 2 (fig. 39). In addition, there were examples of his forms D.2 (from N–U–Forecourt); J (from N–U–5); M.1 (from N–U–5); and L.1 (also N–U–5).

This sample is, of course, too small to allow generalizations about his various categories or ware descriptions, and the reader is referred to his report for further details.

Figure 40 shows several sherds and vessels of a form not found in any of Adams', Shinnie's, or Emery-Kirwan's reports. The small spouted vessel from A–M–4, although somewhat like Adams' L.4, is smaller, more finely made,

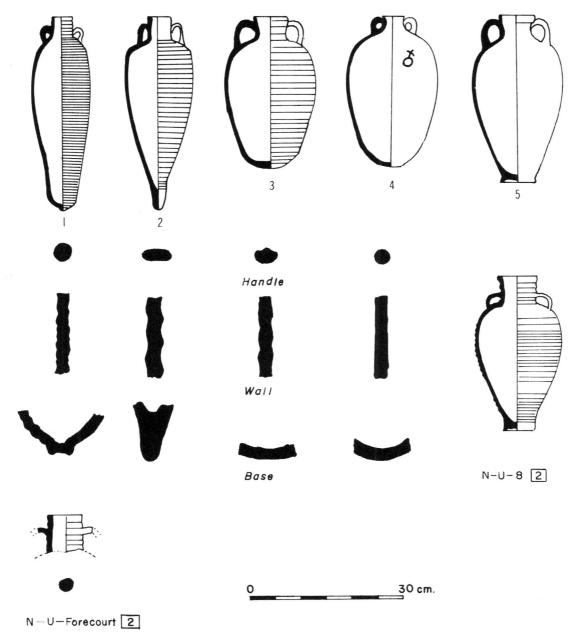

Fig. 36. Christian pottery form class "P": Amphorae

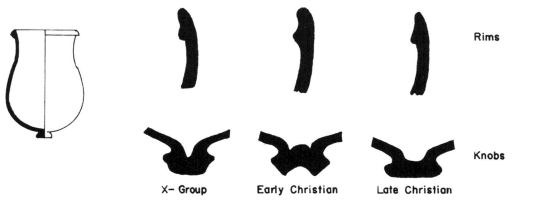

Rims

Knobs

X- Group          Early Christian          Late Christian

Fig. 37. Christian pottery form class "R": *Qadus*

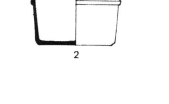

1

2

0                                    20 cm.

Fig. 38. Christian pottery form
class "S": Basins

Emery-Kirwan X.xiii-a
A-M-6 ②
0                    5cm.

Shinnie B-1
N-U-5 ②

0                    5cm.

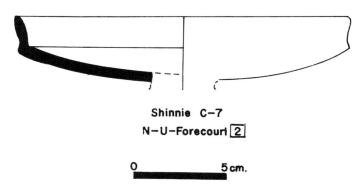

Shinnie C-7
N-U-Forecourt ②

0                    5 cm.

Fig. 39. Vessel types found at Arminna not included in Adams' ceramic typology
(after Shinnie and Chittick, *Ghazali*, figs. 7, 8, and Emery and Kirwan, *Excavations and Survey*, pl. 40)

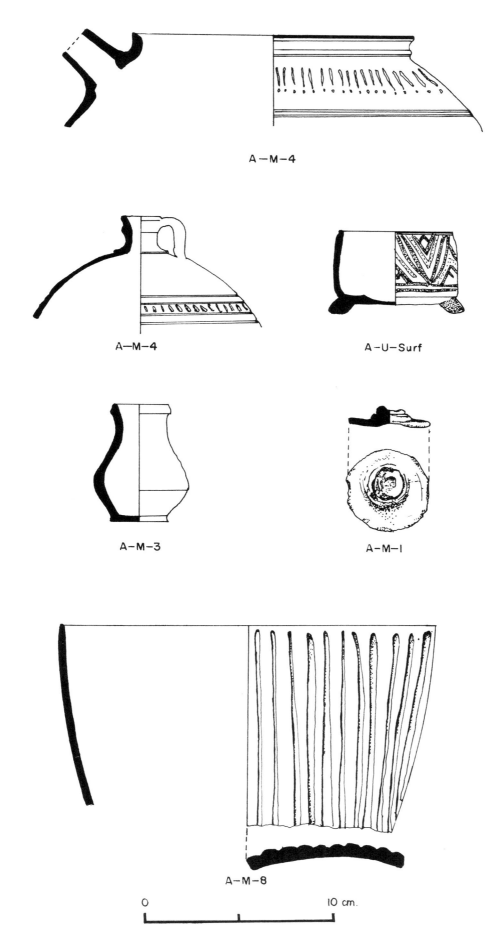

A—M—4

A—M—4

A—U—Surf

A—M—3

A—M—I

A—M—8

0                    10 cm.

Fig. 40. Vessel types found at Arminna not included in previous typologies

TABLE 16. Percentage Distribution of Christian Red Wares by Ware and Form Class at Arminna West, based upon a Sample of *ca.* 1000 Sherds and Vessels

| Ware Number and Name | Frequency | Date | Arminna West Site Levels | A | B | C | D | E | F | G | H | J | K | L | M | N | P | Q | R | S | T | TOTAL[1] |
|---|---|---|---|---|---|---|---|---|---|---|---|---|---|---|---|---|---|---|---|---|---|---|
| 1. Classic X-Group | Abundant | 400–600 | A–M | . | 1.6 | . | 54.2 | 1.1 | . | . | . | . | . | . | * | * | . | . | . | . | . | 57.0 |
| 2. Modified X-Group | Common | 500–700? | A–U, (A–M)[2] | * | 2.7 | 1.1 | 22.4 | 0.3 | * | . | . | . | . | . | * | * | . | . | . | . | . | 26.6 |
| 3. Transitional Red-Orange | Abundant | 500–850 | A–U, (A–M)[2] | . | . | 3.4 | . | 1.1 | . | . | . | . | * | . | . | * | . | . | . | . | . | 4.6 |
| 4. "Samian" Red | Common | 600–750 | A–U, N–U | 0.8 | . | . | . | 1.9 | * | . | . | . | . | . | . | . | . | . | . | . | . | 2.7 |
| 5. Polished Red | Common | 600–850 | A–U, N–U | 0.2 | . | . | . | 2.0 | * | . | 2.0 | . | . | . | . | . | . | . | . | . | . | 4.2 |
| 6. Transitional Soft Red | Common | 600–850 | A–U, N–U | . | * | * | . | 0.8 | . | . | . | . | . | . | . | . | . | . | . | * | . | 0.8 |
| 7. Classic Christian Red | Common | 850+ | A–U, N–U | . | . | 2.2 | . | 3.8 | . | 1.1 | . | . | * | . | . | . | . | . | . | . | . | 7.2 |
| 8. Red Crackled | Very rare | 600–750 | — | . | . | . | . | * | . | . | . | . | . | . | . | . | . | . | . | . | . | 0. |
| 9. Micaceous Red | Very rare | 600–850 | — | . | . | . | . | * | . | . | . | . | . | . | . | . | . | . | . | . | . | 0. |
| TOTALS[1] | | | | 1.0 | 4.3 | 6.7 | 76.6 | 11.0 | | 1.1 | 2.0 | | | | | | | | | | | 100.0 |

FORM CLASSES

[1]Errors in totals are due to rounding.
[2]Levels in parentheses contained only few sherds of the ware.
*Asterisks indicate ware-form combinations noted by Adams but not found at Arminna West.

and with thin walls of a red ware similar to (but not identical with) Adams' wares 4 and 5. The specimen is slipped but not painted and is decorated with incised lines and dots. The small pitcher (A–M–4) is of a similar ware and is decorated in the same fashion. A small bowl (A–U–surface), standing on three legs, is handmade of rather coarse red ware, and painted with red and white designs. The miniature bottle from A–M–3 is also handmade, of a crude, poorly fired red ware. The handmade stopper (A–M–1) is of a ware reminiscent of Early Classic Christian (ware 14). Finally, the red ware vessel from A–M–8 shows deeply incised vertical lines, a rather unusual decorative device for this period.

## II: Wares and Ware Groups

The attributes of any ceramic vessel can be arranged in three general categories: the size and shape of a vessel, or its *form;* its decorative elements, or *style;* and its physico-chemical properties, or *fabric.* These three attribute groups, defined and described by empirical observation, can in turn be placed in statistically defined classes of a more abstract nature. They can form *wares*, which, in Adams' usage, represent "a regular combination of a single fabric, one predominant style (but not excluding others), and a specific group of forms," or, at an even more abstract level, they can form *types*, which represent "a single form occurring in a single ware." Knowledge of X-Group and Christian Nubian pottery is still too incomplete to allow the development of a true typological system, but from his eighteen form classes, ten styles, and five fabrics, Adams has distinguished twenty-seven wares which, in his unpublished *Handbook of Christian Nubian Pottery*, he has arranged in seven ware groups. A brief discussion of these wares and ware groups as they occur at Arminna West follows, and is summarized in Tables 16, 18, 19, and 20.

### Christian Red Wares

I: Classic X-Group. This ware, diagnostic of the X-Group period, occurred in abundance at Arminna, particularly in Form Class "D." There were, however, no examples of larger vessels, i.e., Form Class "M" pots or "N" bottles. In Form Class "D," Ware I paste and slip colors arrange themselves as follows:

TABLE 17. Percentage Distribution of Paste and Slip Colors in Ware I Examples of Form Class "D": Goblets at Arminna West, based upon a Sample of 377 Sherds and Vessels. (Figures are rounded to nearest whole per cent.)

| | COLOR OF SLIP | | | | |
|---|---|---|---|---|---|
| Color of Paste | 10 R 5/4 | 10 R 6/6 | 10 R 4/6 | Other | TOTAL |
| 5 YR 6/6 | 35. | 3. | 2. | 5. | 45. |
| 10 R 6/6 | 24. | 3. | 1. | 3. | 31. |
| 5 YR 7/4 | 1. | 2. | 2. | 2. | 7. |
| Other | 12. | 1. | 1. | 2. | 16. |
| TOTAL | 72. | 9. | 6. | 12. | 100. |

Examples were all of fine textures, well-fired, and generally of medium hardness. Temper was either quartz sand only or quartz sand and mica with occasional small black particles. This is quite in keeping with Adams' description of his Fabric II (called Fabric I: Red-Brown in his *Handbook*).

II: Modified X-Group. Marks the beginning of the Christian period. The ware did not occur in Form Classes "A" or "F" at Arminna West but was found in Form Class "D," a ware-form combination not listed by Adams. Forty per cent of the 200 sherds of this ware and form had a 10 R 6/6 slip, 23% had 10 R 5/4, 15% had 10 R 5/6. Paste was 10 R 6/6 (25%), 5 YR 7/4 (26%), and 5 YR 6/4 (25%). The most frequent combinations were 10 R 6/6 paste with 10 R 5/4 slip, 5 YR 7/4 paste with 10 R 6/6 slip. The sherds and vessels were well-fired, of fine to medium texture, of medium hardness, and normally had quartz sand temper. All examples of Ware II-Form Class "D" came from A–M level 1 or A–U.

III: Transitional Red-Orange. Although described as occurring in abundance from *ca.* A.D. 500–850, specimens of this ware were unusually infrequent at Arminna West (4.6% of all Christian Red wares). Examples were found in Form Classes "C" and "E," but again, as with Ware I, there were no examples in larger vessels (Form Classes "K," "N," and "S"). Specimens seem to occur relatively late, perhaps only during the eighth or early ninth centuries A.D.

IV: "Samian" Red. A "fairly common" ware in smaller vessels from *ca.* A.D. 600–750. Adams notes that this imported Egyptian ware occurs particularly in form E.6 and is the "characteristic ware of the Monastery of Epiphanius at Thebes" during the late VIth and early VIIth centuries. At Arminna West the ware was rare, occurring in Form Classes "A" and "E" in only a very few instances.

V: Polished Red. A local imitation of ware IV, occurring from A.D. 600–850. Although described as common it was fairly rare at Arminna, occurring in only a few examples of Form Classes "A," "E," and "H"; there were no examples in Form Class "F."

VI: Transitional Soft Red. A fairly common ware occurring from A.D. 600–850, particularly in form B.2. At Arminna West the ware occurred only in Form Class "E," and here only in form E.3.

VII: Classic Christian Red. A late (A.D. 850 and later) ware, perhaps fairly common. It was common at Arminna West, occurring in Form Classes "C," "E," and "G." Its occurrence in "E" provides a ware-form combination not listed by Adams.

VIII: Red Crackled. No examples.

IX: Micaceous Red. No examples.

### Christian White Wares

X: X-Group White. A rarely occurring ware from prior to A.D. 400–750. At Arminna West it was rare, occurring in Form Classes "B" and "E" but not in "K" or "M." Ware X in Form Class "B" is a non-Adams combination. Its occurrence in B.5 substantiates the presence of this form before A.D. 1100.

XI: Orange/White. Occurring from A.D. 500–750, this ware is of rare occurrence and, in later times, is easily confused with ware XIX. At Arminna West it was very rare and occurred only in Form Class "E," form E.5.

XII: Transitional White. Adams considers this to be "the most diagnostic ware of the early Christian period"; it occurs from A.D. 500 to 850. In smaller vessels, he states that the slip is cream colored, the decoration of style "f." The earliest examples recorded by him have had a thin white slip and have been rather soft, but the quality of the ware improves through time. At Arminna West, the ware was common, and occurred in Form Classes "A," "B," "C," "E," and "G." The last is a non-Adams ware-form combination, found in G.4. Examples of this ware at Arminna were well-fired, of a fine to medium texture, ranging in hardness from 4 to 9. In Form Class "A" the paste was most frequently 10 R 6/6 or 5 YR 7/4, ranging from a grayish orange pink to grayish orange. The slip was usually 10 Y 8/2, or 10 YR 8/2, with other examples varying from moderate orange pink to very pale orange. The most frequent combinations were a 5 YR 8/4 paste and 10 Y 8/4 slip or 5 YR 7/4 paste and 10 YR 8/2 slip. In Form Class "B" the paste was 5 YR 8/4 or 10 R 6/6, the slip usually 10 YR 8/2 or 10 R 5/4. Form Class "A" sherds were undecorated except for four examples with radial designs (fig. 45), one with an emblem centerpiece, one with interior collar bands of style "g," and one style "f" interior body band. Form Class "B" sherds were undecorated except for one continuous frieze design similar to Adams' style "g-1."

XIII: "Samian" Cream. A comparatively rare ware occurring from A.D. 600–750. It was very rare at Arminna West, occurring only in Form Class "E."

XIV: Early Classic Christian. The origin of this ware, which occurs from A.D. 650 (?) to 750, is unknown. It was rare at Arminna and was found in Form Classes "A" and "G." Its context at the site would suggest that it occurred relatively late (i.e., during the early eighth century).

XV: Classic Christian White. An abundant ware occurring after A.D. 850. It was abundant at Arminna West and occurred in Form Classes "A," "B," "C," and "E." Its occurrence in "B" and "C" represents ware-form combinations not noted by Adams. The forms in which it occurs (B.1, B.2, C.5, and C.6) are all rare during the later periods. This ware most frequently occurred in Form Class "A" at Arminna and, in that form class, had the following characteristics:

Paste: Color usually 5 YR 8/4 to 10 R 6/6, range from 5 YR 6/4 to 10 YR 8/2. Hardness varied from medium (4–6) to hard (7–9); temper was most usually sand (occasionally quartz) or mica, but occasionally with ground sherds mixed with either of the former. Firing was generally of good quality and even throughout the cross section. Texture was fine to medium.

Slip: In over 50% of the cases, the slip was 10 YR 8/2, and this occurred most frequently on saucers with a 5 YR 8/4 or 10 YR 7/4 paste. There were also examples (18% of the cases) of a 10 YR 7/4 slip. Other specimens ranged from 5 YR 7/4 to 10 YR 8/6.

Decoration was most frequently in style "g" but some examples of "h" were present. Radial patterns and emblem or stamped centerpieces were particularly common, and several examples are shown in figs. 44 and 45.

TABLE 18. Percentage Distribution of Christian White Wares by Ware and Form Class at Arminna West, based upon a Sample of ca. 2000 Sherds and Vessels

| Ware Number and Name | Frequency | Date | Arminna West Site Levels | FORM CLASSES | | | | | | | | | | | | | | | | | | TOTAL[1] |
|---|---|---|---|---|---|---|---|---|---|---|---|---|---|---|---|---|---|---|---|---|---|---|
| | | | | A | B | C | D | E | F | G | H | J | K | L | M | N | P | Q | R | S | T | |
| 10. X-Group White | Rare | –400–750 | A–M | . | 2.5 | . | . | 1.2 | . | . | . | . | . | . | * | . | . | . | . | . | . | 3.7 |
| 11. Orange/White | Rare | 500–750 | A–M | . | * | . | . | 0.3 | * | . | . | . | . | . | . | . | . | . | . | . | . | 0.3 |
| 12. Transitional White | Abundant | 500–850 | A–U, A–M | 6.2 | 3.7 | 2.7 | . | 5.8 | * | 1.5 | . | * | . | * | . | . | . | . | . | . | . | 19.8 |
| 13. "Samian" Cream | Rare | 600–750 | A–U, N–U | . | . | . | . | 0.6 | . | . | * | . | . | . | . | . | . | . | . | . | . | 0.6 |
| 14. Early Classic Christian | Very rare | ?650–750 | A–U, N–U | 0.6 | . | . | . | . | . | 0.9 | . | . | . | . | . | . | . | . | . | . | . | 1.5 |
| 15. Classic Christian White | Abundant | 850+ | A–U, N–U | 18.0 | 1.9 | 1.2 | . | 6.2 | . | . | . | . | . | . | . | . | . | . | . | . | . | 27.2 |
| 16. Classic Christian Yellow | Abundant | 850+ | A–U, N–U | 4.6 | 2.7 | 4.6 | . | 19.2 | . | 9.0 | 2.7 | . | . | . | . | . | . | . | . | . | . | 43.0 |
| 17. Christian Heavy Decorated | Rare | 850+ | N–U | . | . | . | . | . | . | 3.1 | . | . | . | . | . | . | . | 0.9 | . | . | . | 4.0 |
| 18. Plain Soft White | Very rare | ?650–850 | — | . | . | . | * | * | . | . | . | . | . | . | . | . | . | . | . | . | . | 0. |
| 19. Hard White | Rare | 600–850 | A–U | * | . | 1.5 | . | * | . | . | . | . | . | . | . | . | . | . | . | . | . | 1.5 |
| 20. Polished Yellow | Rare (?) | 850+ | N–U | 0.3 | . | . | . | 1.2 | . | . | . | . | . | . | . | . | . | . | . | . | . | 1.5 |
| TOTALS[1] | | | | 29.7 | 10.9 | 10.0 | . | 34.5 | . | 14.5 | 2.7 | . | . | . | . | . | . | 0.9 | . | . | . | 100.0 |

[1]Errors in totals are due to rounding.
*Asterisks indicate ware-form combinations noted by Adams which are not found at Arminna West.

TABLE 19. Percentage Distribution of Christian Utility Wares by Ware and Form Class at Arminna West, based upon a Sample of ca. 600 Sherds and Vessels

| Ware Number and Name | Frequency | Date | Site Levels | FORM CLASSES | | | | | | | | | | | | | | | | | | TOTAL[1] |
|---|---|---|---|---|---|---|---|---|---|---|---|---|---|---|---|---|---|---|---|---|---|---|
| | | | | A | B | C | D | E | F | G | H | J | K | L | M | N | P | Q | R | S | T | |
| 21. X-Group Brown Utility | Common | –600 | A–M | . | . | . | . | . | . | . | . | . | . | . | . | . | . | . | 8.1 | * | . | 8.1 |
| 22. Imported Pink Utility | Abundant | 500–750 | A–M | . | . | . | . | . | . | . | . | . | * | . | . | 16.2 | . | . | . | . | . | 16.2 |
| 23. Imported White Utility | Rare | 400–550 | A–M | . | . | . | . | . | . | . | . | . | . | . | . | 0.9 | . | . | . | . | . | 0.9 |
| 24. Imported Brown Utility | Common | 600–750 | A–U, A–M | . | . | . | . | . | . | . | . | . | . | . | . | 3.6 | . | . | . | . | . | 3.6 |
| 25. Christian Red Utility | Abundant | 600–1100 | A–U | . | . | . | . | . | . | . | . | 13.5 | 4.5 | 12.6 | 5.4 | 5.4 | . | . | 9.1 | 5.4 | . | 55.9 |
| 26. Hard Gray Utility | Rare (?) | +1100 | — | . | . | . | . | . | . | . | . | . | . | * | * | . | . | . | . | . | . | 0. |
| 27. Coarse Domestic | Abundant | All | A–U, A–M | . | . | * | . | . | . | . | . | 2.8 | 3.6 | 8.1 | 8.1 | 0.9 | . | . | . | . | . | 15.4 |
| TOTALS[1] | | | | . | . | . | . | . | . | . | . | 2.8 | 13.5 | 13.5 | 13.5 | 26.1 | . | . | 17.2 | 5.4 | . | 100.0 |

[1]Errors in totals are due to rounding.
*Asterisks indicate ware-form combinations noted by Adams which are not found at Arminna West.

XVI: Classic Christian Yellow. Adams distinguishes three types of ware 16: Classic Christian Yellow (ware 16a); Classic Christian Pink (16b); and Chalky White (16c). All forms occur after A.D. 850 in abundance. At Arminna West, ware 16 accounted for 43% of all Christian White wares, and occurred in Form Classes "A," "B," "C," "E," "G," and "H." In Form Class "A," 9% of ware 16 sherds were 16a. All were evenly fired, of medium texture, with sand and/or mica temper. The majority of these sherds had either a 10 YR 8/4 or 5 YR 7/4 paste and a 10 YR 8/2 slip. In Form Classes "B" and "C" the proportion of 16a was similar to that of "A," and the fabric description was the same, although Form Class "B" examples most frequently had a 5 YR 8/4 paste with a 10 YR 8/2 slip or a 5 YR 7/4 paste with a 10 YR 7/4 slip. The remainder of the specimens were ware 16b. In Form Classes "E," "G," and "H," the majority of examples were 16a and again approximated the description of Form Class "A" examples. It should be noted that Adams considers 16a to be confined to northern Nubia and to be replaced by ware 15 in the south.

XVII: Christian Heavy Decorated. A relatively rare ware occurring after A.D. 850. At Arminna West it occurred in Form Classes "G" and "Q" and was not particularly common. Specimens were of medium to coarse texture, rather unevenly fired, with temper of quartz sand and black particles, or quartz sand, mica, and sherds. Paste was frequently 5 YR 7/4 or 10 YR 6/2; slip was generally 10 YR 8/6 or 10 YR 7/4. The majority of specimens came from room N–U–8 level 2.

XVIII: Plain Soft White. No examples.

XIX: Hard White. Although said to occur from A.D. 600 to 850 in Form Classes "A," "C," "E," and "M," the few examples from Arminna West were exclusively of Form Class "C."

XX: Polished Yellow, or Hard Yellow. Occurring after A.D. 850, Adams remarks that, "as similar pieces do not appear in pottery collections from further south (than Faras), the ware is presumed to have been traded from the north." Examples from Arminna West were not common, and occurred in Form Classes "A" and "E." There were no examples in Form Class "C."

### Christian Utility Wares

XXI: X-Group Brown Utility. Identified only in Form Classes "K," "R," and "T," this ware occurs before A.D. 600. It was common in sites excavated by Adams and at Arminna West, although at Arminna it occurred only in Form Class "R."

XXII: Imported Pink Utility. A "regular utility ware" in all Late X-Group and Early Christian sites, the ware is known only in form P.1, and occurs from A.D. 500 to 750. The ware accounted for 16.2% of all Christian utility ware sherds and vessels at Arminna West. This frequency would suggest relatively extensive trade during X-Group and Early Christian times. (See discussion of Form Class "P" for description.)

XXIII: Imported White Utility. Although quite rare, this is perhaps the most accurately dated ware of early times because of the large number of inscriptions found on specimens of it. The ware is found from A.D. 400–550 and occurs only in amphora form P.3. It was rare at Arminna West.

XXIV: Imported Brown Utility. This ware, occurring only in form P.2, is dated from A.D. 600–750. It is the most common amphora ware from the Monastery of Epiphanius at Thebes and "occurs in great quantities for a brief period in early Christian Nubia." It was fairly common at Arminna West.

XXV: Christian Red Utility. Replacing all previous utility wares in Christian Nubia, the ware occurs in abundance from A.D. 600–1100. It was the most common Christian utility ware at Arminna West, and accounted for 55.9% of all Christian utility ware sherds and vessels. (A brief discussion of the ware as it occurs in Form Class "N" is included in the discussion of that form.)

XXVI: Hard Gray Utility. No examples.

XXVII: Coarse Domestic. A handmade ware which has remained unchanged from earliest times to the present day. It was common at Arminna West, and occurred in Form Classes "J," "L," "M," and "N."

### Ware Groups

In his unpublished *Handbook*, Adams has arranged his twenty-seven wares in seven Ware Groups. Table 20 shows the frequency of these groups at Arminna West and in this section we shall briefly discuss their significance. It should be noted that, included in his list of ware groups, Adams presented several new wares which

TABLE 20. Occurrence of Ware Groups I–V at Arminna West

| Ware Group | Date | Frequency | Arminna West Site Levels | Frequency |
|---|---|---|---|---|
| I | −400–850 | Abundant | A–U, N–U, A–M | Abundant (40.2%) |
| II | −400–750 | (1) | A–U, N–U, A–M | Rare (6.4%) |
| III | −400–750 | Rare | A–U, A–M | Rare (1.7%) |
| IV | +850 | Abundant | A–U, A–M (2) | Abundant (46.2%) |
| V | +1000 | (3) | — | No examples |

(1) Abundant in ware 22; common to rare in others.
(2) Finds in A–M are from upper stratum (level 1) only and are perhaps to be associated with A–U.
(3) Frequency varies considerably with ware.

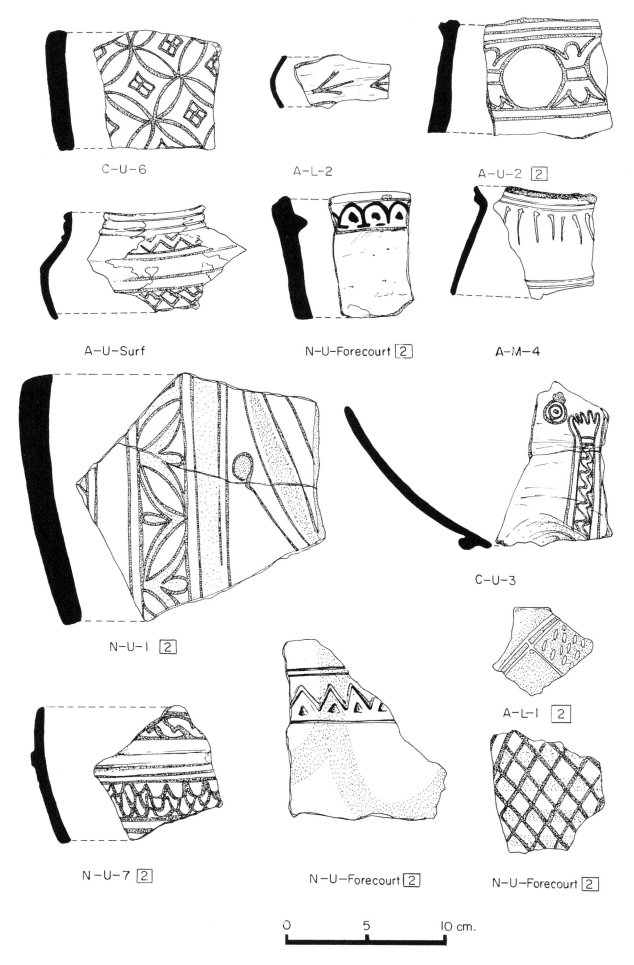

C-U-6  A-L-2  A-U-2 2

A-U-Surf  N-U-Forecourt 2  A-M-4

C-U-3

N-U-1 2

A-L-1 2

N-U-7 2  N-U-Forecourt 2  N-U-Forecourt 2

0       5       10 cm.

Fig. 41. Selected examples of painted wall sherds

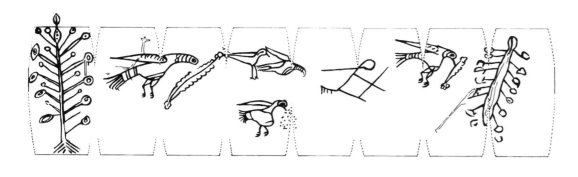

Fig. 42. Painted jar number 309 (*Journal d'Entrée* 89743)

had been set forth after publication of his initial "Classification." References to these new wares, descriptions of which were not available, have been omitted from this study.

Ware Group I: X-Group and Early Christian Native Nubian Wares. Comprises wares 1, 2, 3, 5, 6, 11, 12, 19, and 21; occurs in abundance in all Early Christian sites from the First to the Fourth Cataracts. Fabric is derived from Meroitic pottery but form changes; earliest examples are "copied from imported Egyptian prototypes." Abundant at Arminna West. Adams suggests that the "remarkably consistent and homogenous group, showing no perceptible variation in technique or style throughout the entire area from the First to the Fourth Cataract . . . may point to a very limited number of centres of manufacture."

Ware Group II: Imported Egyptian Wares of the Early Christian Period. Comprises wares 4, 13, and 22; abundant in ware 22, common to rare in others. The Ware Group forms include "A," "E," "F," "H," and P.1. Adams remarks that the presence of numerous examples of P.1 suggests "a very extensive wine trade between Nubia and Upper Egypt throughout the X-Group and early Christian periods." The infrequent occurrence of Ware Group II examples at Arminna West is an important point in this regard (see discussion in Part 1).

Ware Group III: Imported Southern (?) Wares of the Early Christian Period. Comprises wares 10, 14, and 18; rare. For various reasons, Adams ascribes a southern (perhaps Fourth Cataract) origin to this Ware Group. Further, the paucity of finds and consistency of fabric would tend to indicate a single center of origin. Examples of the Ware Group are very rare at Arminna West and occur primarily in area A–M.

Ware Group IV: Classic and Late Christian Native Nubian Wares. Comprises wares 7, 11, 15, 16, 17, 20, and 25; abundant. Adams states that the Ware Group's principal forms include classes "A," "C," "E," and "G." In addition to these, however, sherds and vessels at Arminna West included examples of Form Classes "B," "H," "K," "L," "M," "N," "P," "R," and "S." Adams remarks that the Ware Group shows evidence of influence from the south, is quite heterogeneous and as a consequence difficult to define completely, and suggests several centers of manufacture. This Ware Group was the most frequently found at Arminna West, and accounts for 46.2% of the sherds and vessels. Of all the ware groups, it is this which requires the greatest amount of additional study.

Ware Group V: Imported Egyptian Wares of the Late Christian Period. This Ware Group, which points to trade of varying intensity between Egypt and Nubia after A.D. 1000, was conspicuously absent at Arminna West. Although the Ware Group is not particularly common at any site, its absence is a most important point in reconstructing the history of the site and of Lower Nubia in general during Late Christian times (see Part 1).

Ware Group W: Nubian Women's Handmade Domestic Wares. Adams' description of this Ware Group, which includes his Ware 27, was not available during laboratory analysis of the Arminna West material and has therefore been excluded from our discussion. Examples of Ware 27, however, comprised 5.1% of the sherds and vessels from levels A–U and A–M, and were found with varying frequency in Form Classes "C," "J," "L," "M," and "N."

Ware Group X: Unclassified and Uncertain Wares. Again excluded. This group includes wares 8, 9, 23, and 24, all rare or absent at Arminna West, and comprises only 1.5% of the total sherd and vessel population.

### III: A Brief Note on Styles

We have not found it necessary to discuss in detail the Christian Nubian ceramic styles from Arminna West or their relation to forms and wares since the Arminna West material so closely follows Adams' classification. In figures 41–45 and plates X–XII a few of the more interesting specimens are illustrated. The reader is referred to Adams' works for further discussion of similar pottery decorative motifs.

With the exception of two sherds from A–L which are of early X-Group date, and a later X-Group example from A–M, sherds in fig. 41 are of Classic Christian times. Designs occur on Ware 7 sherds and are in red-brown or red-orange.

The vessel shown in pl. Vf (and in fig. 42), now *Journal d'Entree* 89743, was found near the surface in a room south of the large east-west wall which forms the southern boundary of area N. The jar is of Ware 7 and is 47 cm. in height (the mouth has a diameter of 18.5 cm.).

Incised, moulded, and punched designs are shown in fig. 43. Of interest are the examples of roulette tooling (a, c, d, f, etc.), a decorative style which Adams notes is confined to wares 4, 13, 2, and 5.

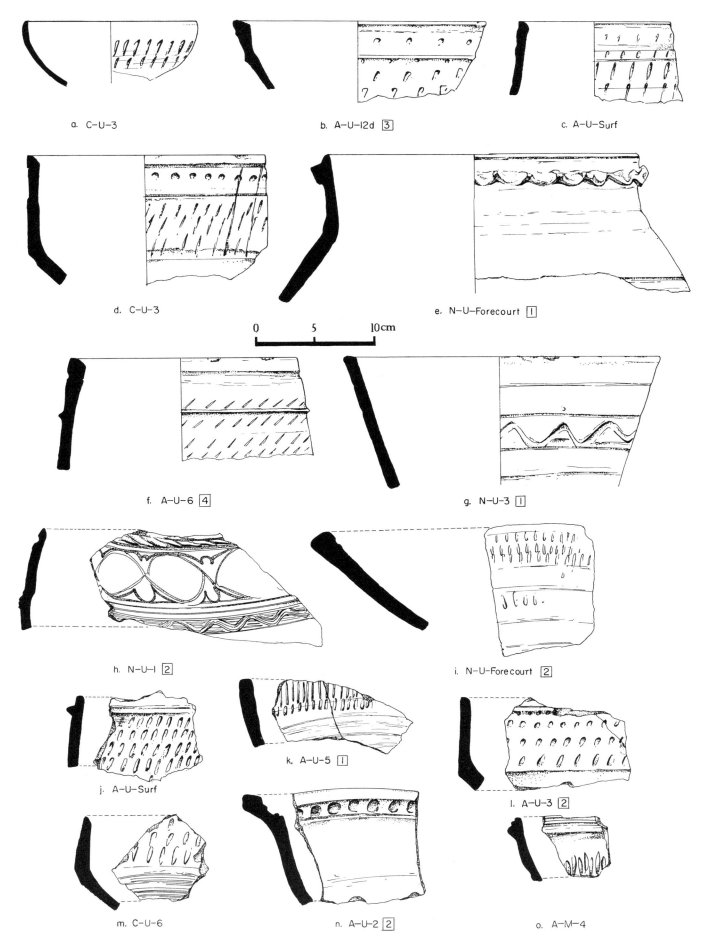

a. C–U–3

b. A–U–12d ③

c. A–U–Surf

d. C–U–3

e. N–U–Forecourt ①

0    5    10cm

f. A–U–6 ④

g. N–U–3 ①

h. N–U–1 ②

i. N–U–Forecourt ②

j. A–U–Surf

k. A–U–5 ①

l. A–U–3 ②

m. C–U–6

n. A–U–2 ②

o. A–M–4

Fig. 43. Incised, impressed, and relief decorations of non-Adams style

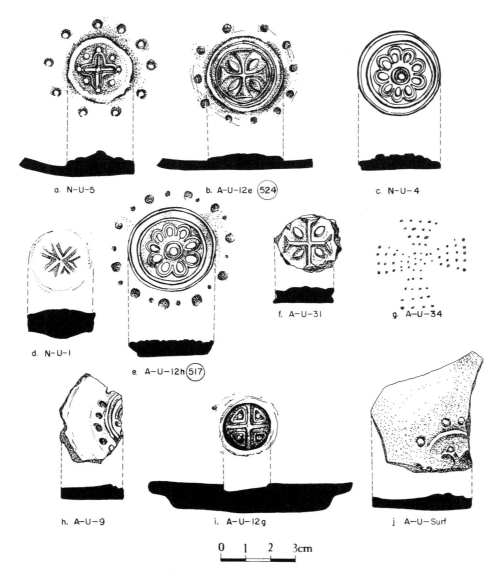

a. N-U-5      b. A-U-12e (524)      c. N-U-4

d. N-U-1      e. A-U-12h (517)      f. A-U-31      g. A-U-34

h. A-U-9      i. A-U-12g      j. A-U-Surf

0   1   2   3cm

Fig. 44. Selected stamped centerpieces

Stamped centerpieces or center seals are particularly common relief decorations during later Christian times and, according to Adams, may represent potter's marks. Over thirty such seals were found at Arminna West, examples of which are shown in fig. 44, pl. XI, and the frontispiece.

Of particular interest are the seals of a helmeted man (frontispiece and pl. XI), similar examples of which have been found at Gebel Adda,[10] at Abka,[11] and at Kerma.[12] Shinnie, commenting upon these latter two specimens,

reads the inscription as oc Pωμα, and describes the pieces as follows:

> The significance of the design and the inscription is obscure. One would like to see in the man's head a representation of a king of Nubia, and such it may well be, but the headdress is one not known from other representations of the Nubian kings; it looks indeed more like the Pope's tiara. The Pωμα of the inscription is presumably Rome, but oc appears to be no known word . . . Perhaps the whole design and inscription is copied from an east Roman original, either a coin, a medallion, or a pot stamp, but no parallels have yet been found.
>
> It may be that the inscription is to be read as Pωμαιος, the demotic equivalent of Pωμαῖος known to designate the Emperor Augustus, but it is difficult to see how such an idea could have survived in the Sudan to the late date at which these roundels must have been made, unless they are indeed degenerate copies of some much earlier medallion.[13]

He tentatively assigns a 9th- or 10th-century date to the specimens.

10. Nicholas B. Millet, personal communication (1965). One example was found, a surface find from the eastern portion of the Citadel. Simpson, *JARCE* III (1964): 16, ftn. notes that "another example is said to have been found in the excavations of the Oriental Institute south of Abu Simbel, and I have been informed that still another example was found in the excavations of the Department of Antiquities at Aswan in the work conducted by Mr. el Hitta."

11. Khartoum Museum number 5383.

12. Khartoum Museum number 5493.

13. Shinnie, *SNR* XXXI (1950): 297–99.

a. A-U-Surf  b. A-U-12a  c. A-U-12d  d. N-U-1

e. N-U-1  f. C-U-8  g. N-U-1  h. N-U-6  i. A-U-Surf

j. A-U-12b  k. N-U-1  l. A-U-Surf  m. N-U-1

n. A-U-12d  p. A-U-Surf  r. A-U-12d

o. C-U-7  q. A-U-37  s. C-U-1

0    5    10cm

Fig. 45. Selected painted centerpieces

Radial patterns and emblem centerpieces (fig. 45) from Arminna West conform to Adams' style "g," found in Ware 14 from A.D. 850–1100 and in locally made wares after that time.

## IV: Observations

It is no doubt apparent from the preceding discussion of the Christian Nubian pottery at Arminna West that the debt owed William Adams by archaeologists engaged in Nubian studies is indeed great. The mere fact that a ceramic classification existed upon which our analysis could be based was in itself of great value. But, furthermore, the methodological approach used in this classification has proved so satisfactory that geographic and chronological observations, so necessary to an understanding of Nubian culture history, can now be made with far greater ease and accuracy than was possible before. Although we at first undertook two separate analyses of the Arminna West material, one independent of Adams' classification, another based exclusively upon it, it became apparent that the latter approach would yield the better data. Only when dealing with fabrics have we found it necessary to depart from his system, in part because of the difficulty of making physico-chemical analyses without samples of his sherds in front of us, in part because of the variability of the sample size with which we dealt. In studying ceramic form classes, our occasional use of other source materials speaks less about the incompleteness of his categories than it does about the geographic variation in ceramic production in Nubia during Christian times.

We have already dealt with the significance of Ware Group frequencies at Arminna West (Part 1) and have discussed the importance of the individual wares themselves. However, several ware-form combinations from Arminna have yet to be noted, combinations which are of some chronological interest.

The presence of form C.7 in ware 16 provides an interesting problem of chronology, since C.7 is said to occur from pre-A.D. 400 to 600 and ware 16 is not noted prior to A.D. 850. The combination of this ware and form at Arminna West (found in *ca.* 30% of all C.7 sherds and vessels) requires an adjustment of these dates, although the combination may well indicate a re-introduction of form C.7 at Arminna West during later times (perhaps only a reflection of the archaizing proclivities of a single workshop) rather than its continuous manufacture throughout the Christian period. A similar adjustment seems necessary to account for examples of B.5 forms in ware 10.

Examples of form G.5 (A.D. 850–1100), a form called "a specialized product of the Classic Christian period," are found with some frequency in ware 14 (A.D. 650?–750). This is particularly intriguing since this ware is one of Adams' mysterious "Imported Southern (?) Wares of the Early Christian Period." The presence of this ware-form combination will have to be identified in other sites before any conclusions can be drawn.

# Chapter Three:

# The Meroitic Pottery

EXCAVATIONS IN LEVEL A–L of the Classic Christian Townsite were not sufficiently complete to allow any detailed analysis of the Meroitic remains from this portion of the Arminna Plain. Material from this period is covered in some detail in the accompanying volume by Bruce G. Trigger[1] and the data recorded in this chapter may be considered an appendix to that report.

The following brief catalogue of Meroitic pottery is based upon the work of W. Y. Adams[2] and of W. B. Emery and L. P. Kirwan.[3] A more detailed analysis of these vessel forms and wares is available in Adams' Meroitic pottery classification.

The principal Meroitic form classes represented in area A–L were Adams' "C," "A," and "K." In addition, however, several examples of Emery and Kirwan's forms W.xxii, W.xxxiv, and W.xlii were recovered.

*Form Class "A": Cups.*

Common, particularly in Classic Meroitic times, but with examples found in later periods as well. Only five examples were found at this part of Arminna, chiefly from A–L–2 level 2.

*Form Class "C": Bowls.*

C.1–4 are not common; the remainder are abundant. At Arminna, C.1 was found in A–M–1 level 3 (1 example), A–L–1 level 2 (3 examples), and A–L–2 level 2 (1 example); C.2 was from A–M–1 level 1 and A–L–1 level 2 (3 examples); C.3; A–L–1 level 3 (2 examples); C.5: 3

examples from A–L–1 level 2; C.7: 4 examples from A–L–1 level 2; others (8 examples) from A–L–1 level 2 and A–L–2 level 2.

*Form Class "D": 'Basins.'*

Common in Meroitic houses. Arminna Townsite yielded five examples, all from A–L–1 level 2.

*Form Class "E": Lekythoi and Small Bottles.*

Only one found at Arminna Townsite, in A–L–1 level 2.

*Form Class "H": Bottles.*

Sub-forms are common to abundant. One example from A–L–1 level 2.

*Form Class "J": Pots and Jars.*

"Fragments of these vessels are quite common in house sites despite the fact that they were designed for use elsewhere."[4] Three examples, from A–L–1 level 2 and A–L–2 level 2.

*Form Class "K": Large Storage Jars.* Common. Five examples from A–L–1 level 2 and A–L–2 level 2.[5]

Examples of Emery and Kirwan's form W.xxii-d came from A–L–1 level 1 and A–L–1 level 3 (one example each). Two examples of W.xlii-c were found, in A–M–1 level 1 and A–L–1 level 1. Most common was W.xxxiv-a, of which twenty examples were found in A–L–1 levels 1 and 2.[6]

1. Trigger, 1967: 59 ff.
2. Adams, *Kush* XII (1964): 126–73.
3. Emery and Kirwan, 1935. See also the chapter on pottery by L. P. Kirwan in Emery 1938.

4. Adams, 1964: 132.
5. The above form class descriptions are based upon Adams, 1964: 130–40, 166.
6. Emery and Kirwan, 1935: I, 512–14 and II: pls. 38–39.

# PART 4

# SMALL OBJECTS

VILLAGE SITES are seldom as productive of bone, clay, or metal as cemeteries and this accounts in part for the paucity of such finds at Arminna West. In addition, however, their absence would seem to indicate a peaceful end to habitation at the site, an end in which there was sufficient time to gather together the various objects and furnishings in the houses before moving elsewhere.

The artifacts are generally of the types one would expect to find in a habitation site, although the small number of beads recovered is somewhat surprising (cf. the large numbers of such objects in the houses at Gebel Adda).

## A. The Ostraca (fig. 46).

Considering the large number of sherds and whole vessels recovered from the Classic Christian Townsite (over 35,000 specimens), the paucity of ostraca is somewhat surprising. Only twenty-six examples were found, one of them (z) painted, the remainder of them scratched on the vessel or sherd. Of these twenty-six examples, the majority represented the name or the monogram ΜιχαΗλ. Exceptions were b (=182?), k (=98?) d and e (=alpha and omega), u (perhaps to be read as Χπθ),[1] and w (palm branches).[2] Several specimens, g, m, o, p, t, and y, were too incomplete to be read, while f, i, and z could not be translated.

## B. Lamps (fig. 47).

Nine lamps were found. By association, all may be assigned a Classic Christian date except c, which may be of Early Christian times. Adams is currently preparing an intensive study of Christian Nubian lamps which should shed light on this most important feature of Christian sites. Until such time as a comprehensive study has been made only brief notes on the Arminna West collection need be given.

Examples of lamps similar to our a, f, and g have been described by Griffith;[3] forms a, b, c, f, and i may be seen in the corpus of Monneret de Villard;[4] see also the brief discussion of lamps (form class "U") in Adams.[5]

## C. Objects of Bone and Clay (fig. 48).

Two bone awls were found in level 2 of room N–U–1. The first (a) is rather crudely made from the ulna of a small mammal and is worked only at the distal end. The piece is 8.4 cm. in length. The second (b) is 11.2 cm. in length and is more carefully made. At its upper end it is 0.4 cm. in diameter, gradually tapering to a fine point. Two deeply incised grooves were made near the head, perhaps for the attachment of thread.

A fragment of bone 5.5 cm. in length (c) was found in level 2 of N–U–Forecourt. The bone had been cut and broken at one end, while the distal end of the fragment had been filed and smoothed to form a curved chisel-shaped edge. Along one side of the piece are a series of incised lines forming a continuous V-pattern.

From below floor III in room A–U–12e a loom weight of lightly fired clay was recovered (e). The piece was 7.2 cm. in length and ca. 1.3 cm. in diameter. At one end a 0.5 cm. hole had been made for attachment of the string or thread. The lower end was slightly flattened, giving the specimen a lenticular cross section.

A lightly fired clay handle (d) was found in the upper stratum of room A–L–2.

A large die, measuring 2.80 x 2.80 x 2.85 cm. was found in level 1 of room N–U–4. Each side had from one to six holes impressed in it. Between the two rows of three holes on one side was a series of thirteen pin pricks, joined by a series of shallow incised lines. The die was well-fired and polished. Whereas the pattern of holes on a contemporary die follows a 1–6, 2–5, 3–4 pattern (the sum of opposing sides always totalling seven), the markings on this specimen are arranged in a 1–6, 2–3, 4–5 series. Whether the small ivory die uncovered by Emery in tomb Q.3–97 at Qustul had similar markings is not known.[6]

A bone lid (g), presumably used for a small jewelry or cosmetic box, was found on the floor of room C–U–3. The piece was 4.3 cm. wide, 5.8 cm. long, and 0.3 cm. thick. A 0.2 cm. deep depression, 3.7 cm. in diameter, had been cut into the underside of the lid, probably to facilitate the small container which the box held. An irregular pattern of incised lines which do not seem to be merely accidental covered the top of the lid.

## D. Objects of Copper and Bronze (fig. 49; pl. XI)

Two bronze knife handles were found, the first (a), from A–U–12h, measuring 11.8 cm. in length, the second (b) from N–U–4, measuring 11.5 cm. Both were badly cor-

---

1. Shinnie and Chittick, 1961: 95.
2. Ibid., p. 103.
3. Griffith, LAAA XIV, nos. 3–4 (1927): 57–116. See especially pls. LVIII and LIX.
4. Monneret de Villard, 1935–57: III, appendix, and IV: pl. 181.
5. Adams, Kush X (1962): 245–88.
6. Emery, 1938: I, 345 and II: pl. 87f.

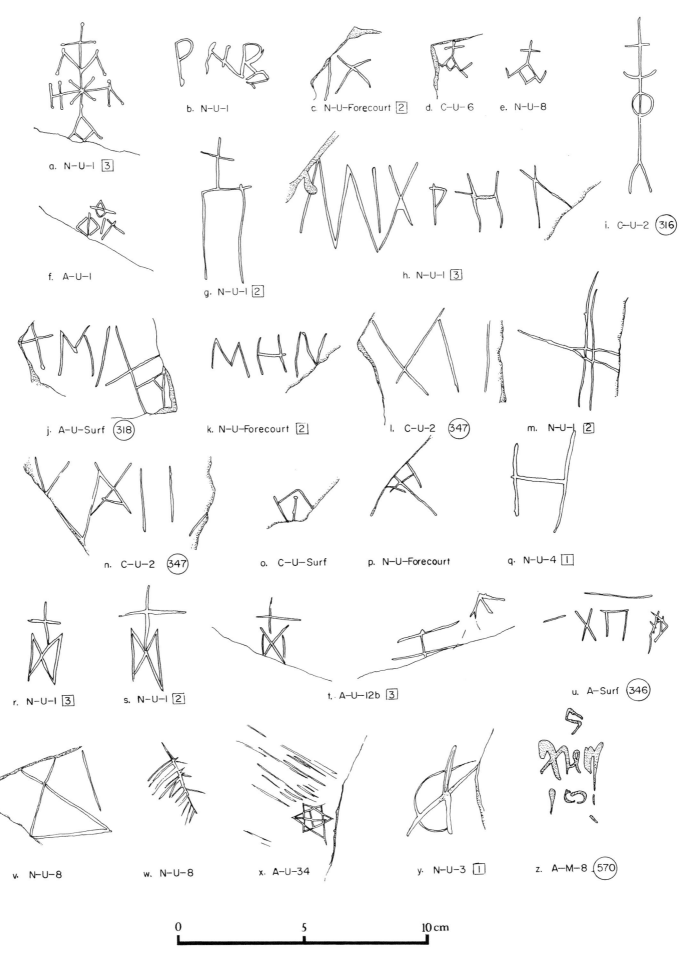

a. N-U-I [3]

b. N-U-I

c. N-U-Forecourt [2]

d. C-U-6

e. N-U-8

f. A-U-I

g. N-U-I [2]

h. N-U-I [3]

i. C-U-2 (316)

j. A-U-Surf (318)

k. N-U-Forecourt [2]

l. C-U-2 (347)

m. N-U-I [2]

n. C-U-2 (347)

o. C-U-Surf

p. N-U-Forecourt

q. N-U-4 [1]

r. N-U-I [3]

s. N-U-I [2]

t. A-U-12b [3]

u. A-Surf (346)

v. N-U-8

w. N-U-8

x. A-U-34

y. N-U-3 [1]

z. A-M-8 (570)

0     5     10 cm

Fig. 46. Christian ostraca

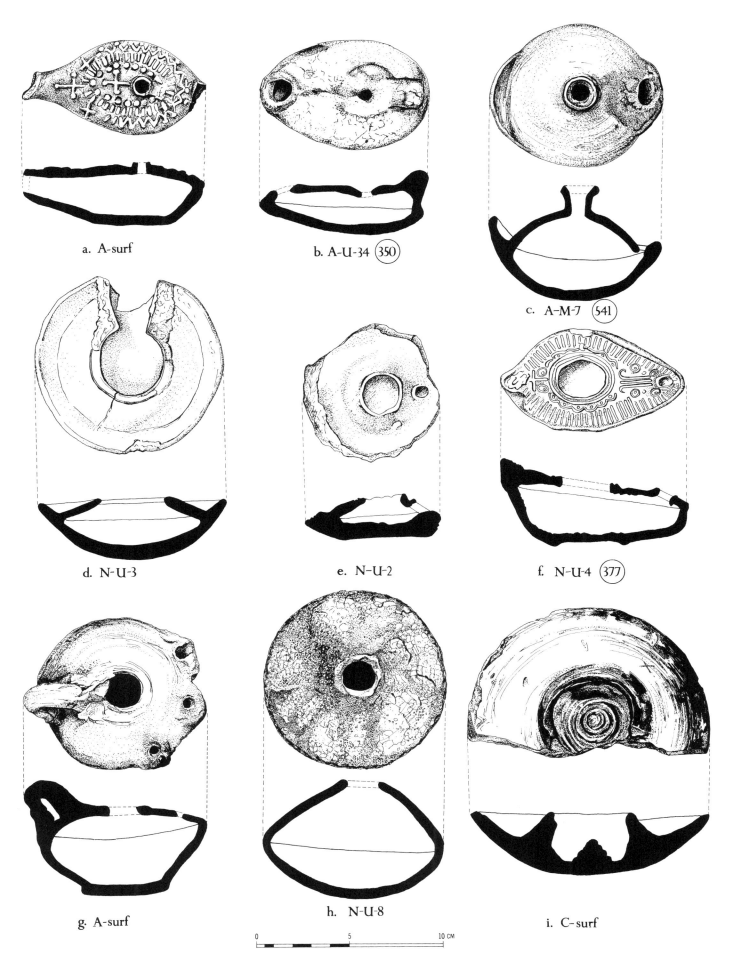

a. A-surf

b. A-U-34 ⃝350

c. A-M-7 ⃝541

d. N-U-3

e. N-U-2

f. N-U-4 ⃝377

g. A-surf

h. N-U-8

i. C-surf

0    5    10 CM

Fig. 47. Pottery lamps of the Christian period

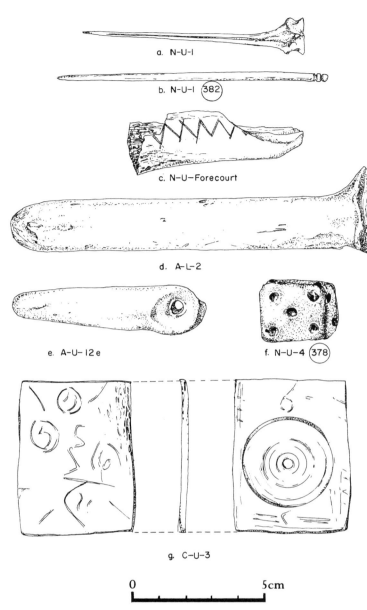

Fig. 48. Artifacts of bone and clay

is 7 cm. in diameter and 5 cm. high, and is decorated with a series of incised parallel lines on its outer surface. There was a small handle or stuck-on relief decorative device near the lip of the cup which had been broken off.

A bronze stamp measuring *ca.* 4.5 x 2.5 cm. was found in level 2 of room A–U–9 (pl. XIe). The piece shows a bird with raised wings and a cross above its head, and probably represents the Holy Spirit. A stamped sherd with a similar decorative device has been described by Arkell[9] from Ain Farah in Darfur.

*E. Objects of Stone* (fig. 50; pl. XI)

A stone stamp, 12.05 cm. long, 3.50 cm. wide and, at its maximum 3.80 cm. high, was found in level 2 of room A–U–5. The bottom of the stamp was covered with a pattern of relief lines, arranged in an alternating sequence of four vertical and two horizontal. The set repeats itself four times on the specimen.

Two incised stone objects were found. The first, from the surface of area A–U appears to be simply a geometric design, the purpose of which is not known. The second, from A–U–34, is incised with the name of Michael and may have been used as a stamp. The latter piece is 7.7 cm. in length and 4.3 cm. wide.

9. Arkell, *Kush* VII (1959): 115–19; see also Trigger, 1967.

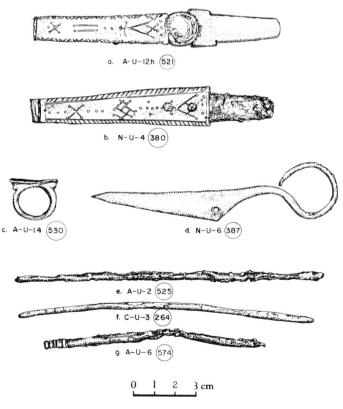

Fig. 49. Artifacts of metal

roded but incised dots and lines were visible on one surface. What these incised decorations represent is not known.

A bronze ring (*c*) was recovered from A–U–14. The bezel is of oval shape and measured 2.4 x 1.2 cm. Unlike those rings illustrated by Emery[7] there is no constricted neck separating the bezel and the hoop, and the specimen is rather more like those reported by Firth.[8]

Three iron kohl applicators (*e, f, g*) and an iron scissor were found in the upper strata of the Upper Building level.

From level 1 of room C–U–1 came a small bronze cup (pl. XIc), unfortunately rather badly preserved. The cup

7. *Ibid.,* II: 42.
8. Firth, *ASN* 1915: pl. 38.

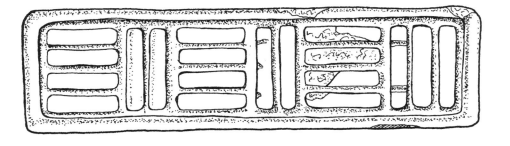
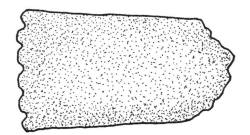

0    1    2    3cm

A–U–5 ⑤⑳

Fig. 50. Stone stamp of the Christian period (room A–U–5)

Fragments of a Coptic tombstone (pl. Xf) were found in level 1 of N–U–4. The text reads as follows:

NTAMI[            ]ⲀⲐⲞⲚⲰ
ⲰⲘⲈ[              ]ⲌⲒⲦⲢⲞ
Nⲓ2Ⲱ[                      ]
ⲢⲨⲞⲨⲈⲒ[          ]ⲘⲈⲚⲦ
[                    ]Ⲁ϶ⲀⲞⲘⲢ
[                    ]ⲢⲀⲤ ⲈⲢⲈ
[                    ]†ⲚⲀϥⲚⲞ
[                    ]ⲚⲀ϶Ⲉ
[                    ]Ⲁ϶Ⲙ
[                  ]2ⲀⲘⲎⲚ†

*F. Other* (figs. 51, 52; pls. XI, XII)

Four fragments of glass vessels were recovered, all from the lower levels of rooms A–U–12 (pl. XId). Some of these may have been used for perfumes or other cosmetics, although the possibility of their being ampullae for the chrism should not be overlooked.[10]

A lightly fired clay Meroitic offering table was found in the fill of room A–M–7b (pl. XIIa).

10. Butler, 1884: II, 56 and fig. 6.

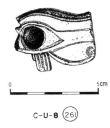

0                    5cm

C–U–8 ㉖

Fig. 51. Faience *uadjet* eye of the Meroitic period (room C–U–8)

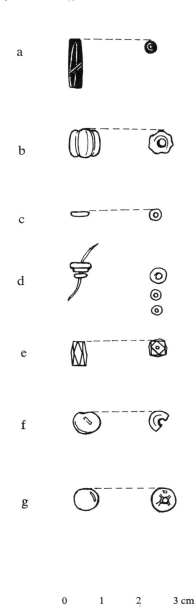

a

b

c

d

e

f

g

0    1    2    3 cm

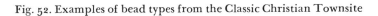

Fig. 52. Examples of bead types from the Classic Christian Townsite

69

## TABLE 21. BEAD CATALOGUE

| TYPE | Material | Size (mm.) | Findspot |
|---|---|---|---|
| a. Cylindrical (round cross-section, length over 1 mm.) | Jasper | 12 × 5 | A–U–1, level 2 |
| | Glass | broken | A–U–9, level 1 |
| | Stone | 7 × 4 | A–U–9, level 1 |
| b. Fluted cylindrical | Faience | 11 × 9 | A–U–11, level 2 |
| | Faience | 10 × 10 | C–U–1, level 2 |
| | Faience | 10 × 9 | N–U–1, level 2 |
| c. Disc-shaped | Faience | 4 × 1 | N–U–Forecourt, level 2 |
| d. Round, flat | Coral | 2 × 1 | A–U–12d, level 3 |
| | Coral (6) | 2 × 1 | A–L–2, level 2 |
| | Faience | 2 × 1 | A–U–12d, level 3 |
| | Faience | 5 × 2 | A–U–5, level 2 |
| e. Biconal | Glass | 6 × 3 | A–Surface |
| f. Round or oval | Glass | 9 × 8 | N–U–3, level 2 |
| | Glass | 6 × 4 | A–U–11, level 2 |
| g. Ball-shaped | Glass | 9 × 7 | C–U–1, level 1 |

A well-made *uadjet* eye, of faience, was found in the lower level of room C–U–8. The piece is of Meroitic date and may well have originally come from cemetery B at Arminna West.

Fragments of a Christian jar seal (pl. Ve) were found near the surface in area "A."

Beads were surprisingly scarce in the Classic Christian Townsite. The few specimens found are briefly described in Table 21.[11]

11. The descriptive classification used here is based upon that of Trigger, 1967. For comparative studies, the drawings accompanying each category should allow reference to Emery, 1938: II, 43–44.

# Index

a

b

c

d

e

f

[Plate I.] General views of the Plain of Arminna

[Plate II.] Classic Christian Townsite, Area A–U, during initial clearing

a    b

c    d

e    f

[Plate III.] Classic Christian Townsite, Upper Building level, structural details

a

b

c

d

e

[Plate IV.] Classic Christian Townsite, "The Public Building"

a  b

c  d

10 cm

e  f

[Plate V.] Classic Christian Townsite, "The Public Building" (a–d) and finds from Upper Building level

a

b

c

[Plate VI.] Classic Christian Townsite, Area C–U

a    b

c    d

[Plate VII.] Classic Christian Townsite, Area C–U

a    b

c    d

e    f

g    h

[Plate VIII.] Classic Christian Townsite, Area N–U

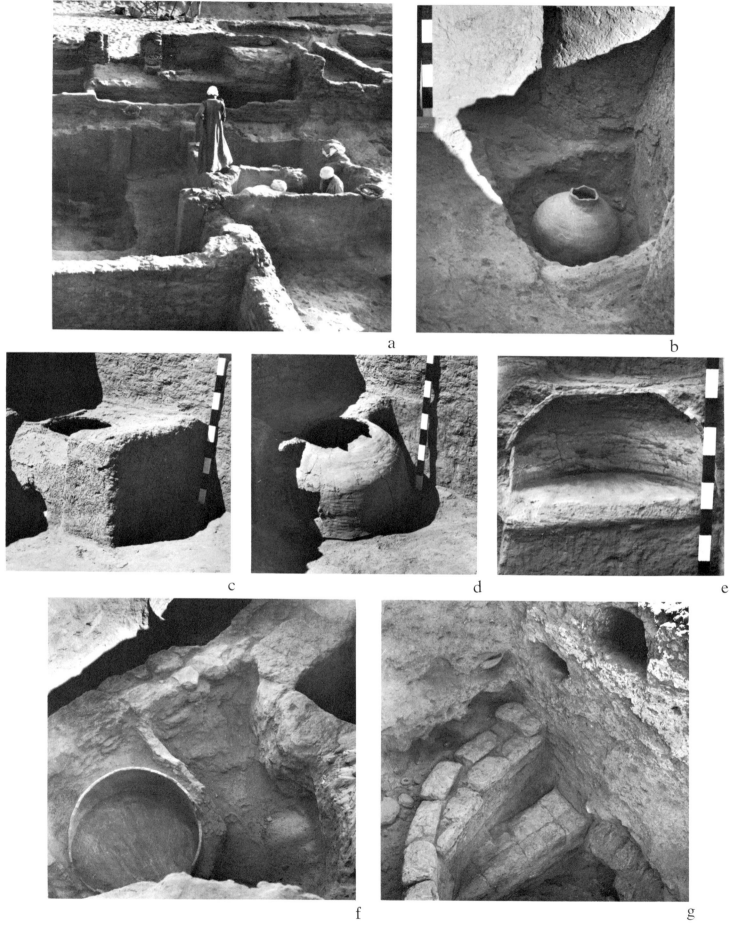

a

b

c

d

e

f

g

[Plate IX.] Classic Christian Townsite, Middle and Lower Buildings levels

a

b

c

d

e

f

[Plate X.] Pottery and stela from Upper Building level

[Plate XI.] Stone, bronze, glass, and pottery artifacts from Upper Building level

a

b

c

d

15 cm

[Plate XII.] Meroitic offering table (a), Meroitic sherds (c–d), and Islamic pottery (b) from Classic Christian Townsite

a

b

c

d

[Plate XIII.] A contemporary Nubian village: Abu Simbel North, 1964